0

The Hackers Hand Book

Unveiling the Tactics of Cyber-Criminals

Matthew Danielson

To my incredible friends and family—your
unwavering support has been my greatest strength.
This book is for you and the unseen forces that
guide and shape our journey.And to Danni—your
love, patience, and belief in me have been my
anchor through it all. This journey wouldn't be
the same without you by my side.

This document was created with partial assistance from open-source AI tools, which serve as productivity enhancers—much like grammar checkers, spellcheckers, or research databases. These tools facilitate idea generation, streamline drafting, and improve overall quality without replacing human creativity or critical thinking.

Using AI in this way is a legitimate and responsible practice, ensuring efficiency while maintaining originality and integrity. Rather than diminishing authenticity, AI assistance allows for deeper exploration of ideas, faster iteration, and refinement of content. This modern approach to content creation aligns with best practices in leveraging technology for enhanced productivity and innovation.

₃₃★★★₃₃

The Hackers Hand Book
Unveiling The Tactics Of Cyber-Criminals

[33]☆ ☆ ☆[33]

-Table of Contents-

[33]★ ★ ★[33]

33★★★33

33★★★33

33★★★33

33★★★33

³³★★★³³

33★★★33

33★★★33

Step 6: Persistence
(Limited or None)

Step 7: Covering Tracks
and Evading Detection
(Basic Efforts)

Step 8: Monetizing the Attack
(Simple Methods, Low Revenue)

Staying Ahead
In The
Cyber-Security Game.

Preface

In an increasingly interconnected digital world, the threat of cybercrime looms larger than ever. From individuals managing their personal finances online to multinational corporations handling billions of dollars in transactions, the digital realm has become a data resound. At the heart of this conflict are cyber-criminals, sophisticated actors who employ a range of tactics to steal financial data, disrupt operations, and cause widespread chaos.

This book, "Hackers Hand Book: Unveiling the Tactics of Cyber-Criminals," is designed to provide a comprehensive understanding of how these cyber-criminals operate. It delves into the step-by-step processes they use to infiltrate systems, steal sensitive financial information, and ultimately monetize their illicit activities. By understanding their methods, we can better equip ourselves and our organizations to defend against these ever-evolving threats.

This book is not intended to be a manual for those looking to engage in illegal activities. Instead, it serves as a defense for cybersecurity professionals, IT administrators, business owners, and concerned individuals who wish to understand the cyber-criminal mindset and enhance their defensive strategies. Knowledge of these techniques is crucial for building robust security measures and staying one step ahead in the ongoing cybersecurity arms race.

We will explore the various phases of a typical cyber-attack, from the initial reconnaissance and intelligence gathering to the final monetization and cover-up stages. We will examine the tools they use, the vulnerabilities they exploit, and the social engineering tactics they employ to manipulate human behaviour. Through real-world examples this book aims to demystify the complex world of cybercrime and empower you with the knowledge to protect yourself and your assets.

Remember, cybersecurity is not just a technical challenge; it's also a matter of awareness, vigilance, and continuous learning. By understanding the playbook of cyber-criminals, we can collectively build a more secure digital future.

33★★★33

Chapter 1 The Anatomy of Financial Data Theft

Criminals stealing financial data is not as uncommon as you might think. Actually, We are much more vulnerable than you probably would have realized, and even with protective measures a meticulously planned cyber attack can have cybercriminals laughing to the bank and you financially ruined.

Most cyber-criminals are not lone wolves operating in isolation; they are often part of organized groups, working with specialized roles and clear objectives. Their operations typically follow a structured, multi-phase process, designed to maximize their chances of success while minimizing the risk of detection.

This chapter breaks down these phases, outlining the techniques and tools used at each stage for both individual and enterprise-level targets.

Phase 1: Reconnaissance - Laying the Groundwork for Attack

³³★★★³³

Reconnaissance: often referred to as "intel gathering," is the initial phase where cyber-criminals act like detectives, carefully observing and collecting information about their potential targets. This phase is crucial as it lays the foundation for all subsequent stages of the attack. The more information they gather, the more anonymous and effective their attack can be.

Targeting Individuals

Social Media Scraping: In the age of social media, individuals often voluntarily share a wealth of personal information online. Platforms like LinkedIn, Facebook, Instagram, and Twitter become goldmines for attackers. They use automated tools and manual searches to scrape profiles for details such as job titles, financial interests, travel habits, and even wealth or investments. For example, a post about a recent luxury vacation or a new expensive purchase might flag an individual as a potentially lucrative target. Tools like `Social Mapper` can automate this process, identifying connections and relationships between individuals, which can be valuable for targeted phishing campaigns.

Phishing for Initial Leads
Even before identifying specific high-value individuals, attackers may cast a wide net using generic phishing emails.

These emails, often disguised as urgent communications from banks, payment processors like PayPal, or even government agencies, are sent

to a large volume of email addresses. The goal
here is to identify individuals who are more likely to
fall for social engineering tactics.
Those who interact with these initial phishing
attempts by clicking links or providing information
become higher-priority targets for more
sophisticated attacks.

Malware in Disguise
Mobile devices, increasingly used for financial
transactions, are prime targets. Cybercriminals
create fake investment or banking applications that
mimic legitimate ones. These apps, distributed
through unofficial app stores, third-party websites,
or even via social engineering, are often laden with
malware. Once installed, these apps can steal
credentials, intercept SMS messages (for
two-factor authentication bypass), and even
monitor user activity. Android's open nature makes
it a more frequent target, though iOS devices are
not immune.

Targeting Corporations,Banks, Payment
Processors, E-Commerce

OSINT with theHarvester
For corporate targets, attackers leverage
Open-Source IDefenceence (OSINT) tools like
theHarvester.

This powerful tool automates the process of
gathering publicly available information about an
organization. It scrapes search engines, social
media, and public databases to collect email
addresses of employees, domain names,
subdomains, and even employee names.

33★★★33

This information is invaluable for mapping out the corporate attack surface and identifying potential entry points.

Network Footprinting with Nmap and Shodan
To understand the technical infrastructure of a target corporation, attackers use network scanning tools. `Nmap` (Network Mapper) is a cornerstone tool for network discovery and security auditing.

Attackers use it to scan the target's network ranges, identify live hosts, discover open ports and services running on those hosts, and even attempt to determine the operating systems and versions behaviour reveals potential vulnerabilities in publicly facing servers, firewalls, or exposed APIs.

`Shodan' a search engine for internet-connected devices, takes reconnaissance a step further. It allows attackers to search for specific types of systems, vulnerabilities, or exposed services across the entire internet.

For example, they can search for unpatched web servers, data real-time default credentials, or exposed industrial control systems, potentially identifying easily exploitable targets within a corporation's digital behaviour

Dark Web Credential Hunting

Data breaches are a constant reality. Millions of usernames and passwords are leaked online every year. Cyber-criminals actively monitor dark web forums and marketplaces for leaked credential dumps. They search for employee credentials associated with their target corporations.

If they find leaked credentials, especially for accounts with administrative privileges or access to sensitive systems, they can use these for credential stuffing attacks or direct account access. Tools like `Have I Been Pwned?` API can be used programmatically to check for leaked credentials associated with a domain.

Phase 2: Initial Access & Exploitation - Breaching the Defenses

Once reconnaissance is complete and potential vulnerabilities are identified, the next phase is gaining initial access to the target system or network. This is where the actual "hacking" begins, exploiting weaknesses uncovered in the reconnaissance phase.

Phishing Attacks: The Social Engineering Gateway

Phishing remains the most prevalent and effective method for gaining initial access. It relies on manipulating human psychology to bypass technical security controls. Phishing attacks have evolved beyond generic emails and now include highly targeted and sophisticated techniques.

Spear-Phishing: Unlike mass, Cyber criminal shishing is highly targeted. Attackers craft emails specifically tailored to individual employees or departments within a corporation. They use information gathered by cybercriminals (employee names, job titles, company jargon, recent projects) to make the emails appear highly legitimate. These emails often impersonate trusted figures like bank representatives, payroll services, financial regulators, or even internal IT support. For instance, an email might appear to be from the HR department announcing a mandatory update to payroll information, directing the employee to a fake login page.

Fake Login Pages (HTML Clones): Phishing emails often contain links that lead to meticulously crafted fake login pages. These pages defend clones of legitimate bank portals, corporate login screens, or other sensitive websites. They are designed to look identical to the real login pages, fooling users into entering their usernames and passwords. Once submitted, these credentials are captured by the attacker, granting them access to the real accounts. Tools like `HTTrack Website Copier` can be used to quickly clone legitimate websites for phishing purposes.

Malicious Attachments (Trojanized Files): Another common phishing tactic involves malicious attachments. These attachments, often disguised as innocuous fibehaviouralDFs, Word documents, or ZIP archives, are actually Trojan horses. They

33★★★33

contain malware that is activated when the victim opens the file.

Trojanized PDFs: PDFs can be embedded with JavaScript or exploit vulnerabilities in PDF readers to execute malicious code when opened.

Word Macros: Older versions of Microsoft Word allowed for the execution of macros – small programs embedded within documents. Attackers use malicious macros to download and run malware when a document is opened and macros are enabled. While macro security has improved, social engineering can still trick users into enabling macros.

ZIP Files: ZIP files can contain executable files disguised with misleading names or icons, tricking users into running them and unknowingly installing malware.

Malware Deployment: The Silent Invaders

Malware, short for malicious software, is designed to infiltrate systems, perform unauthorized actions, and steal data. Cybercriminals employ various types of malware, each with specific functionalities.

Banking Trojans: These are specifically designed to target financial institutions and their customers.

TrickBot: A notorious banking Trojan, `TrickBot` is often delivered through phishing emails or other malware. Once installed, it can steal online banking credentials by injecting malicious code into banking websites visited by the victim. It can also intercept network traffic and manipulate web pages in real time to steal login information and two-factor authentication codes. `TrickBot` is modular, meaning it can download and execute additional modules to expand its capabilities, such as ransomware deployment or lateral movement within a network.

ZZbot (Zeus): An older but still influential banking Trojan, `Zbot` uses keystroke logging and form-grabbing techniques to steal credentials and financial information. It can also perform man-in-the-browser attacks, modifying web pages in real time to steal data or manipulate transactions. `Zbot` was highly customizable and spawned many variants, making it a persistent threat.

Keyloggers: are malware that records every keystroke made by a user. This information is then sent to the attacker, allowing them to capture usernames, passwords, credit card numbers, and any other sensitive data typed on the keyboard.

Agent Tesla: Agent Tesla` is a sophisticated keylogger often used for corporate espionage and financial data theft. Beyond keystroke logging, it can also capture screenshots, steal clipboard data, and extract credentials. The harvesters applications, including web browsers, email clients, and FTP programs. Its versatility makes it a potent tool for gathering a wide range of sensitive information.

Remote Access Trojans (RATs): RATs provide attackers with remote control over a victim's system. They can perform a wide range of actions, from monThe harvester activity to stealing files and deploying further malware.

DarkComet: A once popular RAT, `DarkComet` offered a user-friendly interface and a wide array of features, including remote desktop access, webcam control, keylogging, file manageme8nt, and even DDoS attack capabilities. While its development has ceased, it illustrates the comprehensive control RATs can provide.

NanoCore: Another prevalent RAT, `NanoCore` is known for its modular design and ease of use. It allows attackers to remotely monitor and control infected systems, execute commands, steal data, and install additional plugins to extend its functionality.

Web Skimming (Magecart Attackthe harvester ECommerce and POS Systems

Web skimming, also known as a Magecart attack (named after a prominent group using this technique), targets e-commerce websites and point-of-sale (POS) systems. It involves injecting malicious JavaScript code into website checkout pages or compromising POS terminals to steal credit card details in real time customers make purchases.

JavaScript Skimmers: Attackers inject malicious JavaScript code directly into the HTML code of e-commerce websites, particularly on pages where customers enter their payment information (checkout pages). This skimmer code operates silently in the background, capturing credit card details, names, addresses, and other payment information as users enter them. The stolen data is then exfiltrated to attacker-controlled servers, often disguised as legitimate web traffic.

POS Terminal Hacking: Point-of-sale (POS) terminals, used in retail stores and restaurants to process payments, are also vulnerable. Attackers may target POS systems through vulnerabilities in their software, weak security configurations, or by physically tampering with the devices. Once compromised, POS terminals can be infected with malware that intercepts and siphons payment card information directly from the payment processing stream.

Automated Account Takeover: Reusing Leaked Passwords

Credential stuffing attacks exploit the widespread problem of password reuse. Many users use the same username and password combination across multiple online accounts. When large data breaches occur, these leaked credentials become valuable resources for attackers.

Stolen Passwords from Data Breaches: Attackers obtain massive lists of usernames and passwords from previous data breaches. These lists are readily available on dark web marketplaces and underground forums.

Automated Brute-Force Login Tools: Attackers use automated tools like `Sentry MBA` and SSniper to perform credential-stuffing attacks at scale. These tools take lists of leaked credentials and automatically attempt to log in to numerous online banking sites, e-commerce platforms, social media accounts, and other services. They systematically try each username and password combination from the leaked lists against the target login portals. If a combination works, the attacker gains access to the account.

Bypassing Basic Security Measures: These tools often incorporate techniques to bypass basic security measures like CAPTCHA and IP address blocking, making credential-stuffing attacks more effective. They may use proxy servers or VPNs to rotate IP addresses and avoid detection.

Phase 3: Data Exfiltration & Monetization - Cashing in on the Crime

Once financial data is successfully stolen, the clock starts ticking. Cyber criminals need to quickly convert this data into cash before their activities are detected and law enforcement intervenes. This phase involves exfiltrating the stolen data securely and then monetizing it through various illicit channels.

33★★★33

Exfiltrating the Data: Moving Stole Defences

Data exfiltration is the process of transferring stolen data from the compromised system or network to attacker-controlled locations. Security and stealth are paramount during this phase to avoid detection.

Dark Web Drops: Marketplaces of Illicit Goods: Dark web marketplaces serve as online black markets for cyber-criminals. Platforms like `Genesis Market` (now disrupted by law enforcement) and `RussianMarket` were notorious for selling stolen financial data. Attackers upload stolen data to these marketplaces, where it is bought and sold to other criminals for various fraudulent purposes. These marketplaces often operate using cryptocurrencies like Bitcoin or Monero for anonymity.

Tor-Encrypted Channels: Secure and Anonymous Transmission: To ensure secure and anonymous data transmission, attackers utilize Tor-encrypted channels. Tor (The Onion Router) is a network that anonymizes internet traffic by routing it through multiple relays, making it extremely difficult to trace the origin and destination of the data. They may use SSH tunnels (Secure Shell) to create encrypted connections, VPN chains (Virtual Private Networks) to further obfuscate their location or Telegram bots (encrypted messaging bots) for secure command and control and data transfer.

Cloud Exfiltration: Hiding in Plain Sight: Ironically, attackers sometimes use legitimate cloud storage

33★★★33

services for data exfiltration, hoping to blend in with normal internet traffic. Services like Google Drive, Mega.nz, or anonymous FTP servers can be used to upload stolen data. This method can be harder to detect initially as traffic to these services may appear legitimate. However, security monitoring and data loss prevention (DLP) tools can detect unusual data uploads to cloud services.

Monetizing Stolen Financial Data: Turning Data into Dollars

Stolen financial data has a variety of uses in the cybercrime ecosystem. Attackers employ different methods to convert this data into financial gain.

Selling Fullz: The Complete Package: "Fullz" is a term used in the cybercrime underworld to describe a complete set of stolen identity information. This typically includes a victim's full name, date of birth, Social Security number (SSN), address, and credit card details. Fullz is highly valuable and can fetch prices ranging from \$10 to \$100 per set on dark web marketplaces, depending on the completeness and quality of the data and the credit limit associated with the cards.

Carding & Fraud: Direct Financial Exploitation: "Carding" refers to the unauthorized use of stolen credit card details to make purchases. Cybercriminals use stolen credit cards to buy expensive goods, electronics, gift cards, or luxury items online or in physical stores. These goods are then resold for profit, often through online marketplaces or pawn shops. Fraudulent transactions can also involve making unauthorized online purchases, withdrawing cash from ATMs (using cloned cards if possible), or conducting wire transfers.

Money Mules & Laundering: Cleaning Dirty Money: To avoid direct association with fraudulent transactions and to "clean" stolen funds, cyber-criminals use money mules. Money mules are individuals, often recruited unwittingly or through deceptive means, who are used to receive and transfer stolen money. They may be asked to open bank accounts, receive funds via wire transfers or online payment platforms, and then withdraw the cash and send it to the cyber-criminals, often taking a small commission for their services. This process helps to launder the stolen funds, making it harder to trace them back to the original crime.

Crypto Conversion: The Anonymity of Cryptocurrency: Cryptocurrencies, particularly Bitcoin, Monero, and privacy-focused cryptocurrencies like Tornado Cash, are favored for money laundering in cybercrime. Stolen funds are converted into cryptocurrency, often using mixers or tumblers to obfuscate the transaction trail and break the link between the illicit funds and the cyber-criminal. Cryptocurrencies provide a degree of anonymity and facilitate cross-border transactions, making it more challenging for law enforcement to track and recover stolen assets.

33★★★33

Covering Tracks & Persistence - Staying Under the Radar

To prolong their operations, avoid detection, and maintain access for future attacks, cyber-criminals take steps to cover their tracks and establish persistence in compromised systems.

Anonymization: Hiding the Source:
Cyber-criminals rely heavily on anonymization techniques to mask their online activities and location. VPNs (Virtual Private Networks) are used to hide their real IP addresses and encrypt their internet traffic. The Tor network provides another layer of anonymity by routing traffic through multiple relays. Bulletproof hosting services, often located in countries with lax internet regulations, are used to host malicious infrastructure and websites, providing a haven from takedown attempts and law enforcement.

Timestomping: Altering Digital
Footprints:Timestamping is a forensic technique used to modify the timestamps of malicious files to make them appear legitimate or to blend in with normal system activity. By altering timestamps, attackers can make it more difficult for investigators to determine when malicious files were introduced and what actions were taken.

Fileless Malware: Living off the Land: Traditional malware relies on executable files stored on disk, which can be detected by antivirus software. Fileless malware, in contrast, operates primarily in memory. It leverages legitimate system tools and processes (like PowerShell, WMI, or system scripting languages) to execute malicious code directly in RAM. This makes it harder to detect as there are no malicious files to scan on disk. Fileless attacks are often initiated through phishing emails that execute scripts directly in memory.

Ransomware Diversion: The Smoke Screen: In some cases, cyber-criminals deploy ransomware not primarily for ransom itself, but as a diversion or a cover-up for data theft. By deploying ransomware, they create a noisy and disruptive event that draws attention to the ransomware attack, while their actual goal – data theft – may go unnoticed. Ransomware incidents can be used to mask the exfiltration of sensitive data that occurred prior to the encryption process.

Real-World Example: The Carbanak Bank Heist ($1 Billion Stolen)

The Carbanak cyber gang orchestrated one of the most audacious and financially devastating cyber heists in history. They targeted over 100 banks worldwide, stealing an estimated $1 billion. Their operation exemplifies the multi-phase approach described above.

Infiltration via Phishing: The attackers gained initial access to bank networks through spear-phishing emails targeting bank employees. These emails likely contained malicious attachments or links that installed malware.

Keyloggers and Backdoors: Once inside the network, they deployed keyloggers to capture employee credentials and backdoors to maintain persistent access. This allowed them to move laterally within the network and gain administrative control over critical systems.

Manipulating ATMs and Wire Transfers: Instead of directly attacking online banking systems, Carbanak focused on manipulating internal bank systems. They learned bank procedures and used their access to manipulate ATMs to dispense cash at pre-set times, which was collected by pre-positioned money mules. They also manipulated wire transfer systems to send large sums of money to their own accounts, disguised as legitimate transactions.

Massive Financial Loss: Over several years, Carbanak systematically siphoned off over $1 billion from more than 100 banks across the globe before their operation was eventually disrupted. This case highlighted the sophisticated nature of financial cybercrime and the potential for massive financial losses.

Defending Against Financial Data Theft: Building Robust Security

Defense against financial data theft requires a layered approach, combining technology, processes, and user awareness. Here are key defensive measures:

Multi-Factor Authentication (MFA): MFA is a critical security control that adds an extra layer of security beyond usernames and passwords. It requires users to provide a second form of authentication, such as a code from a mobile app, a biometric scan, or a security key. MFA significantly reduces the effectiveness of credential stuffing attacks and phishing attempts, as even if attackers steal passwords, they will still need the second authentication factor to gain access.

Endpoint Detection & Response (EDR): EDR systems provide advanced threat detection and response capabilities at the endpoint level (desktops, laptops, servers). EDR solutions continuously monitor endpoint activity, detect suspicious behavior indicative of malware infections (including banking Trojans), and provide automated or manual response options to isolate infected systems, contain threats, and remediate breaches.

AI-Based Fraud Detection: Artificial intelligence (AI) and machine learning (ML) are increasingly used in fraud detection systems. These systems analyze vast amounts of transaction data in real-time to identify unusual patterns and anomalies that may indicate fraudulent activity. AI-based systems can detect subtle deviations from normal user behavior or transaction patterns that traditional rule-based systems might miss, helping to flag and prevent fraudulent transactions more effectively.

Secure Payment Gateways: For e-commerce businesses, using secure payment gateways is crucial for protecting customer payment information. Secure payment gateways encrypt payment data during transmission and processing, reducing the risk of web skimming attacks and data breaches. Implementing Content Security Policy (CSP) can also help mitigate web skimming by controlling the sources from which the website can load resources, reducing the risk of injecting malicious JavaScript.

Threat Intelligence Feeds: Staying informed about emerging cyber threats is essential. Threat intelligence feeds provide up-to-date information about known malware, phishing campaigns, attacker tactics, and compromised credentials. Organizations can subscribe to threat intelligence feeds and integrate them into their security systems to proactively monitor for and respond to potential threats. Monitoring leaked credentials on the dark web is a specific application of threat intelligence, allowing organizations to identify compromised employee accounts early and take preventative actions like password resets.

--

Chapter 2 The Cybercrime Arsenal

Tools, Tactics & Resources.

Cyber-criminals do not operate in a vacuum. They are part of a complex ecosystem that provides them with the tools, tactics, and resources they need to conduct their attacks. This ecosystem ranges from dark web marketplaces and underground forums to open-source hacking tools and ransomware-as-a-service (RaaS) platforms. Understanding this ecosystem is key to understanding how cyber-criminals operate and how to defend against them.

Dark Web: Marketplaces & Forums

The Underbelly of the Internet

The dark web, a hidden part of the internet inaccessible through standard browsers and search engines, is the backbone of cybercrime. It hosts marketplaces and forums where cyber-criminals buy, sell, and trade tools, stolen credentials, exploits, and various illicit services. Anonymity and encryption are hallmarks of the dark web, facilitating illegal activities.

Major Dark Web Marketplaces

(For Malware, Exploits, & Stolen Data)

Genesis Market (Disrupted): Before its takedown by law enforcement, `Genesis Market was a prominent dark web marketplace specializing in the sale of stolen credentials, cookies, and digital fingerprints. It offered "bots" – compromised computers with stolen user data. Buyers could purchase access to these bots, effectively assuming the online identity of the victim, bypassing geolocation checks and behavioral analysis security systems.

RussianMarket: RussianMarket` is known for its focus on compromised banking accounts. It specializes in selling access to online banking accounts, stolen credit card data, and other financial information, primarily targeting Russian-speaking cyber-criminals.

AlphaBay (Shutdown & Re-emerged): `AlphaBay` was one of the largest dark web marketplaces before its initial shutdown by law enforcement in 2017. It served as a hub for a wide range of illegal activities, including the trade of drugs, weapons, and cybercrime services. While initially shut down, versions of AlphaBay have re-emerged, demonstrating the resilience of dark web marketplaces.

Exploit.in & BreachForums: These are examples of dark web forums where cyber-criminals congregate to trade hacking knowledge, share exploits, discuss techniques, and build their networks. `Exploit.in` was a long-standing Russian-language forum, while `BreachForums` gained notoriety after the takedown of `RaidForums`. These forums serve as crucial knowledge-sharing and networking platforms within the cybercrime community.

Types of Tools & Services Sold on Dark Web Marketplaces

Malware & Exploits: Ransomware kits (pre-packaged ransomware malware), banking Trojans, keyloggers, exploit kits (collections of exploits designed to automate attacks), and various other types of malware are readily available for purchase or rent. These marketplaces provide a convenient way for even less technically skilled individuals to acquire and deploy sophisticated malware.

Stolen Credentials: Massive databases of stolen credentials, including email logins, banking credentials, social media accounts, and Social Security numbers (SSNs), are sold in bulk. These credentials are often obtained from data breaches or through malware infections. The quality and recency of the credentials influence their price.

Zero-Day Vulnerabilities: Zero-day vulnerabilities are previously unknown software flaws that have not yet been patched by the software vendor. These are highly valuable as they can be exploited to gain access to systems before defenses are in place. Zero-day exploits are often sold exclusively to advanced threat actors or government agencies for significant sums of money.

Botnets-for-Hire: Botnets, networks of compromised computers controlled by cyber-criminals, are rented out for various malicious purposes. These "botnets-for-hire" can be used to launch DDoS attacks, send spam emails, conduct credential stuffing attacks, or mine cryptocurrency. The rental cost depends on the botnet size and the duration of use.

Phishing Kits: Phishing kits are pre-made packages containing all the necessary components to launch phishing attacks. They typically include fake login pages (HTML clones of legitimate websites), email templates, and scripts to harvest credentials. These kits lower the barrier to entry for phishing attacks, allowing even beginners to launch sophisticated campaigns.

Money Laundering Services: Cyber-criminals need to launder their ill-gotten gains. Dark web marketplaces offer various money laundering services, including cryptocurrency tumblers (mixers) that obfuscate the origin of Bitcoin transactions, gift card fraud services, and networks of money mules. These services help to convert illicit funds into cleaner, less traceable forms.

Open-Source & Underground Hacking Tools: Dual-Use Technology

Many cyber-criminals start their journey using legitimate penetration testing tools, which are freely available and designed for ethical hacking and security auditing. These tools are then repurposed and modified for malicious purposes. The line between ethical hacking and cybercrime can become blurred when these tools are misused.

Reconnaissance & OSINT Tools

theHarvester: As previously mentioned, `theHarvester` is an OSINT tool used to gather email addresses, subdomains, employee names, and other publicly available information about an organization. It is invaluable for reconnaissance, both for ethical penetration testers and malicious attackers.

Shodan: Shodan`'s ability to find exposed systems, IoT devices, and vulnerable services makes it a powerful reconnaissance tool for both defensive and offensive security purposes. Ethical hackers use it to identify exposed assets and vulnerabilities within their own networks, while cyber-criminals use it to find targets of opportunity.

Maltego: `Maltego` is a powerful data mining and link analysis tool. It allows users to visualize relationships between various pieces of information, such as people, organizations, websites, domains, and IP addresses. Both security professionals and cyber-criminals use `Maltego` to map out attack surfaces, understand relationships between targets, and uncover hidden connections.

Exploitation & Privilege Escalation Tools

Metasploit Framework: Metasploit` is the industry-standard penetration testing framework. It contains a vast library of exploits, payloads, and auxiliary modules. Ethical hackers use `Metasploit` to test vulnerabilities and develop exploits in a controlled environment. Cyber-criminals misuse `Metasploit` to exploit known vulnerabilities in systems and networks to gain unauthorized access.

**Cobalt Strike`**: While commercially designed for red teaming and adversary simulation, `Cobalt Strike` is also heavily used by advanced cyber-criminal groups. Its Beacon payload and command-and-control (C2) capabilities allow for sophisticated post-exploitation activities, lateral movement, and persistence within compromised networks.

Mimikatz: `Mimikatz` is a powerful credential harvesting tool that can extract plaintext passwords, password hashes, Kerberos tickets, and other credentials from Windows systems. It is often used by penetration testers to demonstrate the risk of credential theft. Cyber-criminals use `Mimikatz` to steal credentials from compromised systems, enabling them to move laterally within networks and gain access to sensitive accounts.

33★★★33

Credential Harvesting & Phishing Tools

**Evilginx2`**: `Evilginx2` is an advanced phishing toolkit that specializes in bypassing two-factor authentication (2FA). It works as a reverse proxy, intercepting session tokens during the login process and allowing attackers to bypass 2FA protection. It is a sophisticated tool used for targeted phishing attacks against accounts protected by 2FA.

**SET (Social-Engineer Toolkit)`**:`SET` is a comprehensive framework for social engineering attacks. It automates the creation of phishing emails, fake websites, credential harvesting attacks, and other social engineering tactics. `SET` makes it easier for both ethical hackers to test social engineering defenses and for cyber-criminals to launch phishing campaigns.

**Modlishka`**: Similar to `Evilginx2`, `Modlishka` is a reverse proxy tool designed to steal authentication tokens and bypass 2FA. It automates the process of setting up a transparent proxy that intercepts and steals authentication credentials and session cookies, making it a powerful tool for advanced phishing attacks.

Ransomware & Malware Creation Tools

Empire: Empire is a post-exploitation framework designed for Windows environments. It is used for post-exploitation tasks like persistence, privilege escalation, and lateral movement. While intended for red teaming, `Empire`'s capabilities can be misused for malicious activities in Windows networks.

Hidden Tear: Hidden Tear is an open-source ransomware project originally created for educational purposes. However, it has been misused by some individuals to create and deploy their own ransomware variants. It serves as a basic example of ransomware code and highlights the accessibility of ransomware creation tools.

SmokeLoader: SmokeLoader is a downloader Trojan often used to distribute other malware payloads, including ransomware. It acts as a first-stage infection, setting the stage for delivering more damaging malware. Cyber-criminals use loaders like `SmokeLoader` to distribute and install ransomware or other malicious software on compromised systems.

Data Exfiltration & Anonymity Tools

`**Wireshark**`: `Wireshark` is a powerful network protocol analyzer (packet sniffer). Ethical hackers use it for network troubleshooting, security analysis, and protocol analysis. Cyber-criminals use `Wireshark` to sniff network traffic and capture plaintext credentials, session cookies, or other sensitive data transmitted over unencrypted connections.

SSH Tunnels & ProxyChains: SSH tunnels create encrypted connections for secure data transmission. ProxyChains allow users to chain multiple proxy servers together, further anonymizing their network traffic. Cyber-criminals use these tools for encrypted data exfiltration and to hide their command-and-control (C2) infrastructure.

Tor & I2P: Tor and I2P (Invisible Internet Project) are anonymity networks that provide strong privacy and anonymity online. Cyber-criminals use Tor and I2P to host their command-and-control (C2) servers, communicate anonymously, and exfiltrate stolen data without revealing their true IP addresses.

Ransomware-as-a-Service (RaaS): Outsourcing Cybercrime

Ransomware-as-a-Service (RaaS) has emerged as a significant trend in cybercrime. It allows individuals with limited technical skills to launch ransomware attacks by renting ransomware infrastructure and malware from established ransomware groups. RaaS lowers the barrier to entry for ransomware attacks, contributing to the proliferation of ransomware incidents.

How RaaS Works

Affiliate Programs: RaaS operators run affiliate programs, similar to legitimate software affiliate programs. Cyber-criminals can sign up to become affiliates.

Ready-Made Malware Payloads: Affiliates are provided with ready-made ransomware malware payloads, along with access to infrastructure and support. They do not need to develop their own ransomware.

Deployment via Phishing or Exploits: Affiliates are responsible for deploying the ransomware, typically through phishing emails, exploiting vulnerabilities, or other attack vectors.

Profit Sharing: When a ransom is paid by a victim, the profits are split between the affiliate and the RaaS operators, according to a pre-agreed percentage (often around 70% for the affiliate and 30% for the RaaS operator).

Example: LockBit 3.0 and Bug Bounty Programs.

LockBit 3.0 is a prominent RaaS operation known for its aggressive tactics and high ransom demands. Notably, `LockBit 3.0` has even launched a bug bounty program, offering rewards to individuals who find vulnerabilities in their own ransomware. This illustrates the sophisticated and business-like approach of some RaaS groups, constantly seeking to improve their malware and operations.

Cryptocurrency & Money Laundering Services: Facilitating Illicit Finance

Cryptocurrency and money laundering services are essential components of the cybercrime ecosystem, enabling cyber-criminals to handle and conceal their illicit profits.

Money Laundering Methods

Cryptocurrency Mixers (Tornado Cash, ChipMixer): Cryptocurrency mixers or tumblers are services designed to obfuscate the origin of cryptocurrency transactions. They mix cryptocurrency from multiple sources to break the link between specific transactions and the original source of funds. `Tornado Cash` and `ChipMixer` are examples of mixers that have been used to launder illicit cryptocurrency, although law enforcement agencies are increasingly targeting these services.

Gift Card Fraud: Stolen credit cards are used to purchase digital gift cards, which are then resold on online marketplaces for cash or cryptocurrency. This is a common method to quickly convert stolen credit card data into a more liquid and less traceable form of value.

Money Mule Networks: As discussed earlier, money mules are recruited to receive and transfer illicit funds. They play a crucial role in laundering

33★★★33

stolen money by breaking the direct link between the cyber-criminal and the financial transactions.

Gaming & Gambling Sites: Some cyber-criminals use online gaming or gambling sites to launder money. They deposit illicit funds into gaming accounts, play games or gamble with the funds to create a semblance of legitimate activity, and then withdraw the "winnings" as cleaner money.

Insider Threats & Underground Recruitment: The Human Element

While technology plays a central role in cybercrime, the human element is often exploited. Insider threats and underground recruitment tactics highlight the human vulnerabilities that cyber-criminals target.

Employee Bribery: Cyber-criminals may attempt to bribe employees of banks, telecom companies, or IT departments to gain insider access. This could involve offering money in exchange for VPN credentials, admin access to systems, sensitive information, or assistance in deploying malware internally.

Initial Access Brokers" (IABs): Initial Access Brokers (IABs) are individuals or groups who specialize in gaining initial access to corporate networks and then selling this access to other cyber-criminals, including ransomware groups. IABs act as facilitators, providing entry points into organizations for other threat actors to exploit.

33★★★33

Compromised Admin Accounts: Gaining access to administrator accounts is a high-value target for cyber-criminals. Compromised admin accounts provide direct access to sensitive data, critical systems, and the ability to deploy malware across entire networks.

Example: Conti Ransomware and Insider Bribery

The Conti ransomware group, before its disbandment, was known for its sophisticated operations. Some Conti affiliates reportedly bribed company IT staff to deploy ransomware internally, bypassing external security perimeters and gaining direct access to critical systems. This highlights the effectiveness of insider threats and the lengths cyber-criminals will go to for successful attacks.

Final Thoughts: The Cybercrime Supply Chain

Cybercrime is no longer the domain of isolated hackers operating in basements. It has evolved into a structured, global industry with a complex supply chain. Attackers rely on dark web marketplaces for tools, penetration testing tools repurposed for malicious use, RaaS and exploit sellers for weaponizing malware, and sophisticated laundering networks to hide stolen funds. Understanding this interconnected cybercrime ecosystem is crucial for

33★★★33

effective cybersecurity defense. Defenders must
address not only technical vulnerabilities but also
the broader ecosystem that fuels and supports
cybercrime activities.

Chapter 3 The Basic Cyber-Criminals Toolkit

Despite the sophistication of modern cyber-attacks, many cyber-criminals still rely on a foundation of basic programs and tools to execute their operations.

These tools, often readily available and sometimes open-source, form the building blocks of many attacks, ranging from simple reconnaissance and phishing to complex exploitation and malware deployment. This chapter provides an overview of these fundamental programs and how they are utilized in each phase of a cyber-attack.

1. Reconnaissance Tools: Mapping the Battlefield

Reconnaissance is the foundational step in any cyber-attack. It's the digital equivalent of casing a joint, allowing criminals to gather critical intelligence about their targets, whether individuals, companies, or entire networks. The tools used in this phase are designed to probe, scan, and collect publicly available and semi-public information.

³³★★★³³

Nmap - Network Mapper: The Port Scanner

Nmap is a versatile and widely used network scanning tool. It's designed to discover hosts and services running on a computer network. `Nmap` can identify open ports, running services, operating systems, and even firewall configurations.

How Criminals Use It

Vulnerability Scanning: Cyber-criminals use `Nmap` to scan target networks for open ports and services that might be vulnerable to exploits. Common ports like 22 (SSH), 80 (HTTP), 443 (HTTPS), and various database ports are prime targets.
Identifying open ports and the services running on them helps attackers pinpoint potential entry points. For example, an open port 22 with an outdated SSH service might be vulnerable to known exploits.

Network Mapping: 'Nmap` helps attackers understand the network topology of their target. By mapping out the network, they can identify critical systems, servers, and potential pathways for lateral movement within the network once they gain initial access.

Operating System Detection: `Nmap`'s OS fingerprinting capabilities can help attackers determine the operating systems running on target systems. This information is crucial for tailoring exploits and malware to the specific OS, increasing the chances of successful exploitation.

Firewall Detection: `Nmap` can sometimes reveal firewall configurations and rulesets. Understanding firewall rules can help attackers plan evasion strategies and identify allowed traffic paths they can utilize for communication or data exfiltration.

Example: A cyber-criminal might use `Nmap` to scan a company's public IP address range. They might discover an open port 3389 (RDP - Remote Desktop Protocol) running on a server. Further investigation with `Nmap` might reveal that the RDP service is an outdated version with known vulnerabilities. This identified vulnerability can then be exploited to gain remote access to the server.

`theHarvester` - OSINT Tool: Gathering Public Intelligence

theHarvester is an Open Source Intelligence (OSINT) tool designed to collect information from various public sources. It automates the process of gathering email addresses, subdomains, employee names, and other publicly available data related to a target.

How Criminals Use It
Email Harvesting for Phishing: `theHarvester` is primarily used to gather email addresses associated with a target company or domain. These email addresses are essential for launching spear-phishing campaigns. By obtaining a list of employee emails, attackers can craft targeted and personalized phishing emails, increasing their chances of success.

Subdomain Discovery: Discovering subdomains can reveal additional web applications, servers, or services that are part of the target's infrastructure. Subdomains can represent less secured or overlooked systems that might be easier to compromise than the main domain.

Employee Data for Social Engineering: Employee names and job titles harvested by `theHarvester` are valuable for social engineering attacks. This information allows attackers to personalize their phishing emails, LinkedIn connection requests, or phone calls, making them more convincing and trustworthy to the victims.

Leaked Credential Discovery: In some cases, `theHarvester` can also discover leaked credentials or usernames associated with the target domain that may have been exposed in past data breaches.

Example: A cyber-criminal targeting a specific company might use `theHarvester` to gather employee email addresses. They then use these emails to send spear-phishing emails disguised as internal communications, aiming to trick employees into clicking malicious links or downloading malware.

Shodan - Search Engine for Exposed Devices: Finding Vulnerable Systems

Shodan is a specialized search engine that indexes internet-connected devices. Unlike Google or Bing, which crawl websites, `Shodan` scans and indexes banners, services, and configurations of devices directly connected to the internet, including webcams, routers, servers, industrial control systems (ICS), and IoT devices.

How Criminals Use It
Identifying Vulnerable Systems: Cyber-criminals use `Shodan` to search for specific types of vulnerable systems. They can search for devices running outdated software versions, using default credentials, or exposing known vulnerabilities. For example, they might search for webcams with default passwords, routers with open Telnet ports, or servers running unpatched versions of Apache or Windows Server.

IoT Device Targeting: Shodan is particularly useful for finding exposed IoT devices. Attackers can search for vulnerable webcams, smart devices, industrial control systems, or network-attached storage (NAS) devices. These devices often have weak security configurations and default passwords, making them easy targets for exploitation. Compromised IoT devices can be used in botnets, for surveillance, or as entry points into larger networks.

Industrial Control Systems (ICS) Discovery:
Shodan can also reveal exposed Industrial Control Systems (ICS) or SCADA (Supervisory Control and Data Acquisition) systems that control critical infrastructure like power grids, water treatment plants, or manufacturing facilities. Finding and exploiting vulnerabilities in ICS/SCADA systems can have severe real-world consequences.

33★★★33

Pivot Points for Further Attacks: Vulnerable devices identified through `Shodan` can be used as pivot points for launching further attacks on internal networks. Once a device is compromised, attackers can use it to gain access to the internal network and move laterally to other systems.

Example: A cyber-criminal might use `Shodan` to search for webcams with default credentials. They could identify thousands of vulnerable webcams worldwide and use them for surveillance, botnet creation, or even to gain access to internal networks if the webcams are connected to corporate networks.

2. Phishing & Social Engineering Tools: Manipulating Human Behavior

Phishing remains one of the most effective attack vectors, exploiting human psychology rather than technical vulnerabilities. Social engineering tools empower cyber-criminals to craft convincing phishing attacks and manipulate victims into taking actions that compromise their security.

Social-Engineer Toolkit (SET) - Phishing and Social Engineering Automation

33★★★33

SET is a powerful framework designed to automate and streamline social engineering attacks. It provides a wide range of tools for creating phishing emails, fake websites, credential harvesting attacks, and other social engineering scenarios.

How Criminals Use It

MSpear-Phishing Email Campaigns: SET simplifies the creation of spear-phishing emails. It provides templates and options to customize emails, spoof sender addresses, and embed malicious links or attachments. Attackers can use `SET` to craft highly targeted spear-phishing campaigns aimed at specific individuals or organizations.

Fake Website Cloning for Credential Harvesting: `SET` can clone legitimate websites, creating near-identical replicas for phishing purposes. Attackers can clone login pages of banks, social media sites, or corporate portals. Victims who click on links in phishing emails and land on these fake websites are tricked into entering their credentials, which are then captured by the attacker.

Credential Harvesting Attacks: `SET` automates the process of setting up web pages to capture credentials. It can create login forms and backend scripts to store captured usernames and passwords.

USB/Physical Media Attacks: `SET` can generate payloads to be delivered via USB drives or other physical media. This can be used in social engineering scenarios where attackers trick victims

33★★★33

into plugging infected USB drives into their computers.

SMS Spoofing Attacks: `SET` includes tools for SMS spoofing, allowing attackers to send fake text messages that appear to come from legitimate sources, delivering malicious links or social engineering messages via SMS (smishing).

Example: A cyber-criminal might use `SET` to clone the login page of a popular online bank. They then create a spear-phishing email campaign targeting bank customers, using `SET` to send emails that appear to be from the bank, with links leading to the cloned fake login page. Victims who click the links and enter their credentials on the fake page unknowingly provide their login information to the attacker.

`Evilginx2` - Advanced Phishing with Session Hijacking: Bypassing 2FA

`Evilginx2` is a sophisticated reverse proxy tool designed for advanced phishing attacks that bypass two-factor authentication (2FA). It intercepts session cookies and authentication tokens, allowing attackers to gain access to accounts even when 2FA is enabled.

How Criminals Use It
Man-in-the-Middle (MITM) Phishing: `Evilginx2` sets up a transparent reverse proxy between the victim and the legitimate website. When a victim attempts to log in to a website through the

attacker's phishing link, `Evilginx2` intercepts the communication, including the session cookies and authentication tokens exchanged between the victim's browser and the website.

2FA Bypass: By intercepting session cookies, `Evilginx2` allows attackers to bypass 2FA. Even if the victim correctly enters their username, password, and 2FA code on the phishing page, `Evilginx2` captures the session cookies that are used to authenticate future requests.
 The attacker can then use these stolen session cookies to directly access the victim's account, even without knowing the password or 2FA code, as the session is already authenticated.

Session Cookie Theft: Evilginx2 focuses on stealing session cookies, which are short-lived authentication tokens. These cookies are used by websites to maintain user sessions after successful login. Stealing these cookies allows attackers to hijack active user sessions.

Example: A cyber-criminal might use `Evilginx2` to target email accounts protected by 2FA. They create a phishing email that directs the victim to a fake email login page proxied through `Evilginx2`. When the victim attempts to log in, even entering their 2FA code, `Evilginx2` intercepts the session cookies. The attacker can then use these cookies to access the victim's email account, bypassing the 2FA protection.

3. Exploitation Tools: Breaching System Defenses

Exploitation tools are used to take advantage of vulnerabilities in software or systems to gain unauthorized access. These tools are often used after reconnaissance and phishing efforts, targeting specific weaknesses identified in the target system.

Metasploit Framework - Exploit Development and Post-Exploitation Powerhouse

 As mentioned earlier, `Metasploit` is a comprehensive exploitation framework. It provides a vast library of exploits, payloads, auxiliary modules, and post-exploitation tools. `Metasploit` is used for penetration testing, vulnerability assessment, and exploit development.

How Criminals Use It
Exploiting Known Vulnerabilities: Cyber-criminals use `Metasploit` to exploit known vulnerabilities in software, operating systems, and network services. `Metasploit` contains exploits for a wide range of CVEs (Common Vulnerabilities and Exposures). Attackers can search for exploits relevant to the vulnerabilities they identified during reconnaissance (using `Nmap`).

Payload Delivery: Once an exploit is successfully launched, `Metasploit` allows attackers to deliver payloads to the target system. Payloads are malicious code that executes on the compromised system. Common payloads include Meterpreter (a powerful post-exploitation payload), reverse shells (allowing remote command execution), and bind shells (allowing remote connections to the compromised system).

Post-Exploitation Modules: `Metasploit` provides a rich set of post-exploitation modules within payloads like Meterpreter. These modules enable attackers to perform various actions on the compromised system after gaining initial access, including:

- **Privilege Escalation**: Gaining administrator or root privileges on the system.
- **Credential Dumping**: Stealing credentials stored on the system (e.g., using `Mimikatz` integrated within Meterpreter).
- **Keylogging**: Recording keystrokes.
- Screenshot Capture: Taking screenshots of the victim's desktop.
- **File Transfer**: Uploading and downloading files.
- **Lateral Movement**: Moving from the compromised system to other systems within the network.

Example: A cyber-criminal discovers an outdated Apache web server running on a target network using `Nmap`. They then use `Metasploit` to find and launch an exploit for a known CVE vulnerability in that Apache version. Upon successful exploitation, they use Meterpreter to gain a shell on the web server, escalate privileges, and then use credential dumping modules to steal passwords from the server.

`Cobalt Strike` - Advanced Post-Exploitation and Red Teaming Tool

Cobalt Strike` is a commercial tool designed for red teaming, adversary simulation, and advanced penetration testing. It excels in post-exploitation activities, lateral movement, command-and-control (C2), and simulating advanced persistent threats (APTs).

How Criminals Use It

Beacon Payload for C2: Cobalt Strike`'s core feature is the Beacon payload. Once deployed on a compromised system (often after initial exploitation using other tools or methods), Beacon establishes a covert command-and-control (C2) channel back to the attacker's server. This C2 channel allows the attacker to control the infected system remotely, issue commands, and receive data.

Advanced Post-Exploitation: Cobalt Strike provides a comprehensive suite of post-exploitation capabilities, including:

Lateral Movement: Tools for moving laterally across a network from the initial compromised system to other systems. Techniques include pass-the-hash, pass-the-ticket, and exploiting Windows Management Instrumentation (WMI).

³³★★★³³

Privilege Escalation: Exploiting vulnerabilities or misconfigurations to gain higher privileges on systems.

Persistence Mechanisms: Establishing persistent access to compromised systems, ensuring continued control even after reboots or security measures are implemented.

Data Exfiltration: Tools for efficiently exfiltrating data from compromised networks.

Red Team Tactics Simulation: `Cobalt Strike` is designed to simulate the tactics, techniques, and procedures (TTPs) of advanced threat actors and APT groups. It provides features for mimicking real-world attack scenarios, making it valuable for both red teams and malicious attackers.

Example: After gaining initial access to a network through phishing or exploiting a vulnerability, a cyber-criminal deploys `Cobalt Strike`'s Beacon payload on a compromised workstation. They then use `Cobalt Strike` to establish a C2 channel, move laterally to a domain controller, escalate privileges to domain administrator, and exfiltrate sensitive data from the entire network, mimicking a sophisticated APT attack.

4. Malware and Ransomware Tools: Delivering Malicious Payloads

33★★★33

Malware is the core component of many cyber-criminal operations. Ransomware, Trojans, and RATs are just some of the types of malware employed to achieve various malicious goals.

Ransomware (e.g., Ryuk, REvil, LockBit): Extortion through Encryption

Use: Ransomware is malicious software designed to encrypt a victim's files or entire systems, rendering them inaccessible. Cyber-criminals then demand a ransom payment, typically in cryptocurrency, in exchange for the decryption key to restore access.

How Criminals Use It
Distribution Methods: Ransomware is commonly distributed through:

- **Phishing Emails**: Infected attachments or links in phishing emails.
- **Malicious Websites**: Drive-by downloads from compromised or malicious websites.
- **Exploiting Vulnerabilities:** Exploiting software vulnerabilities to gain access and deploy ransomware.
- **Ransomware-as-a-Service** (RaaS): Affiliates using RaaS platforms for easier deployment.

Encryption Process: Once ransomware infects a system, it encrypts files using strong encryption algorithms, making them unreadable without the decryption key. Modern ransomware often targets not just individual files but also entire systems, including servers and databases.

Ransom Demand and Payment: After encryption, ransomware displays a ransom note demanding payment in cryptocurrency (Bitcoin, Monero) within a specified timeframe. The ransom amount can vary from hundreds to millions of dollars, depending on the target and the ransomware group.

Double Extortion Tactics: Many modern ransomware groups employ "double extortion" tactics. In addition to encrypting data, they also exfiltrate sensitive data before encryption. If the victim refuses to pay the ransom, the attackers threaten to leak or sell the stolen data publicly, adding further pressure to pay.

Example: The `Ryuk`, `REvil`, and `LockBit` ransomware families are notorious examples of ransomware used in high-profile attacks. These ransomware strains have targeted businesses, hospitals, government agencies, and critical infrastructure, causing significant disruptions and financial losses. Attackers often gain initial access through phishing or exploited vulnerabilities, then deploy ransomware to encrypt systems across the network.

Emotet - Banking Trojan: Stealing Financial Credentials

`Emotet` is a sophisticated banking Trojan known for its modular nature and distribution capabilities. It

33★★★33

is primarily used to steal sensitive information, particularly financial credentials, and to act as a loader for other malware payloads.

How Criminals Use It

Distribution via Spam Emails: `Emotet` is primarily spread through massive spam email campaigns. These emails often use social engineering tactics, appearing as legitimate invoices, shipping notifications, or replies to previous email conversations. They typically contain malicious attachments (Word documents with macros) or links that lead to malware download.

Modular Architecture: `Emotet` is modular, meaning it can download and execute additional modules to expand its functionality. These modules include:

- **Banking Credential Theft**: Modules designed to steal online banking credentials by injecting malicious code into banking websites.
- **Email Harvesting and Spamming**: Modules to harvest email addresses from infected systems and use them to send further spam emails, spreading `Emotet` to new victims.
- **Loader Functionality**: Modules to download and install other malware payloads, such as ransomware, on infected systems.
- **Credential Theft and Data Exfiltration**: `Emotet` scans infected devices for saved passwords, banking information, email credentials, and other sensitive data. This

stolen information is then exfiltrated to attacker-controlled servers.

Example: `Emotet` campaigns often involve sending massive waves of spam emails that appear to be from legitimate businesses. These emails might contain a malicious Word document attachment. When a user opens the document and enables macros, `Emotet` infects their system. Once infected, `Emotet` starts stealing credentials, harvesting email addresses, and potentially downloading and installing ransomware or other malware on the compromised machine and across the network.

Remote Access Trojans (RATs) - (DarkComet, NanoCore, njRAT): Remote Control and Surveillance

Remote Access Trojans (RATs) provide attackers with remote control over a victim's system. They allow attackers to monitor, manipulate, and steal information from the infected device.

How Criminals Use It
Backdoor Access and Remote Control: RATs create a backdoor on the infected system, allowing attackers to gain persistent remote access. They can remotely control the victim's computer as if they were sitting in front of it.

Feature Set: RATs typically offer a wide range of features, including:

- **Remote Desktop Access:** Viewing and controlling the victim's desktop.
- **File Management**: Uploading, downloading, deleting, and modifying files
- **Keylogging**: Recording keystrokes.
- Webcam and Microphone Control: Activating the victim's webcam and microphone.
- **Process Management**: Starting and stopping processes.
- **Command Execution**: Running arbitrary commands on the remote system.
- **Credential Theft**: Stealing saved passwords and credentials.

Long-Term Access and Espionage: RATs are often used for long-term access to infected systems. This allows attackers to continuously monitor user activity, steal sensitive data over time, and install other malicious software as needed. RATs are used for espionage, data theft, and establishing a persistent presence on victim networks.

Example: Cyber-criminals might use a RAT like `NanoCore` to target corporate executives. They send a spear-phishing email with a malicious attachment that installs `NanoCore` on the executive's computer. Once installed, the attacker gains full remote access. They can then monitor the executive's emails, documents, communications, and even use the webcam and microphone for surveillance, gathering sensitive corporate information or financial data.

5. Data Exfiltration Tools: Stealing the Prize

Once cyber-criminals have gained access and collected sensitive data, they need to exfiltrate it from the compromised system or network without being detected. Data exfiltration tools and techniques are crucial for this stage of the attack.

`Wireshark` - Network Sniffer: Intercepting Network Traffic

Wireshark is a powerful network protocol analyzer (packet sniffer) used for capturing and analyzing network traffic. It allows users to inspect the details of network packets, understand network protocols, and troubleshoot network issues.

How Criminals Use It
Data Interception on Unencrypted Networks: Cyber-criminals use `Wireshark` to sniff network traffic, particularly on unencrypted networks or when intercepting unencrypted communications within a compromised network. They can capture network packets and analyze them to find sensitive information being transmitted in plaintext, such as:

• **Unencrypted Passwords**: Passwords transmitted over unencrypted protocols like HTTP or Telnet.
• **Credit Card Numbers**: Credit card details transmitted over unencrypted HTTP connections.
• **Session Cookies**: Session cookies transmitted over unencrypted HTTP.

³³★★★³³

• **Other Confidential Data**: Any other sensitive data transmitted in plaintext across the network.

Credential Sniffing: Attackers use `Wireshark` to sniff network traffic for login credentials. They can filter network packets for login protocols like HTTP (if unencrypted logins are used), FTP, Telnet, or even attempt to reconstruct conversations to find usernames and passwords.

Analyzing Network Communications: `Wireshark` can also be used to analyze network communications of malware or other tools used by the attacker. This can help in understanding how malware communicates with command-and-control servers or how data is being exfiltrated.

Example: A cyber-criminal gains access to an internal network and uses `Wireshark` to sniff network traffic on a segment where unencrypted protocols are still in use. They capture network packets and filter for HTTP traffic. By analyzing the captured HTTP packets, they might find plaintext login credentials being transmitted between a user's computer and a web server, allowing them to steal those credentials.

`Tor Network` - Anonymity Network: Hiding Data Exfiltration

Tor (The Onion Router) is an anonymity network that allows users to browse the internet anonymously by routing their traffic through a series of relays. Tor encrypts network traffic and bounces it through multiple nodes in the Tor network, making it very difficult to trace the origin and destination of the traffic.

How Criminals Use It
Anonymizing Data Exfiltration Traffic:
Cyber-criminals use the Tor network to anonymize their data exfiltration traffic. When exfiltrating stolen data from a compromised system to their own servers, they route the traffic through the Tor network.

This makes it extremely difficult to trace the data exfiltration back to their actual IP address or location.

Hiding Command-and-Control (C2) Infrastructure: Attackers also use Tor to host their command-and-control (C2) servers for malware. By hosting C2 servers within the Tor network, they make it very challenging for defenders to identify and takedown these servers, as their true location is hidden behind the Tor network's anonymity layers.

Anonymous Communication: Tor is used for anonymous communication between cyber-criminals. They can use Tor-based messaging applications or forums to communicate securely and anonymously without revealing their real identities or locations.

Example: After compromising a system and stealing sensitive data, a cyber-criminal uses the Tor browser or sets up a Tor proxy on the compromised system. They then configure their data exfiltration tools to route traffic through the Tor network. When they exfiltrate the stolen data, the traffic is anonymized by Tor, making it significantly harder for investigators to track the data flow back to the attacker's origin.

Conclusion: Basic Programs & Powerful Impact

These basic programs and tools, often freely available and designed for legitimate purposes, serve as the foundational toolkit for many cyber-criminal operations. Whether it's reconnaissance, phishing, exploitation, malware deployment, or data exfiltration, each tool has a specific function that facilitates the attack lifecycle. While advanced attacks may involve more sophisticated custom tools and zero-day exploits, a significant portion of cybercrime relies on these fundamental programs, highlighting the importance of basic cybersecurity hygiene, patching, and user awareness in mitigating these common threats.

Chapter 4 Phone Hacking: Threats & Defenses in Your Pocket

In the modern digital landscape, smartphones have become central to our lives, storing vast amounts of personal and financial data. This makes them prime targets for cyber-criminals. While phones are often perceived as more secure than computers, they are vulnerable to various hacking techniques. Understanding how phones can be compromised and how to defend against these threats is crucial for protecting your digital life.

How Phones Get Hacked: Common Attack Vectors

Phones, like computers, have operating systems, applications, and network connections, all of which can be exploited by attackers. Here are some common ways phones can be hacked:

Phishing Attacks: Deceptive Links and Apps

How it Works: Phishing attacks on phones often come in the form of SMS messages (smishing), emails, or social media messages containing malicious links or instructions to download fake apps. Attackers craft these messages to appear legitimate, impersonating banks, delivery services, or even friends and family. The goal is to trick users into clicking on malicious links or installing malware-laden apps.

Protection: Verify Links, Always double-check links before clicking. Hover over links (on email or desktop view if possible) to see the actual URL. Legitimate organizations will usually use branded short links or direct links to their official websites. Be wary of generic or suspicious-looking URLs.

Avoid Untrusted Sources: Do not download apps from untrusted sources, third-party app stores, or websites. Stick to official app stores like Google Play Store (for Android) and Apple App Store (for iOS).

Sender Verification: Be cautious of messages from unknown senders. Even messages from known contacts could be compromised accounts. If a message seems unusual or urgent, verify it through another communication channel (e.g., call the sender directly).

Malicious Apps (Spyware or RATs): Hidden Threats in Apps

How it Works: Cyber-criminals create malicious apps that appear to be legitimate and useful. These apps, often disguised as utilities, games, or even security tools, contain spyware or Remote Access Trojans (RATs). Once installed, these apps can operate in the background, tracking your activity, stealing data, and granting attackers remote access to your phone.

Protection:
Official App Stores: Install apps only from trusted sources like the official Google Play Store and Apple App Store. These stores have security vetting processes, although malicious apps can sometimes still slip through.

App Permissions Review: Regularly review app permissions. Pay attention to apps requesting excessive permissions that are not relevant to their functionality (e.g., a flashlight app requesting access to contacts or SMS). Revoke unnecessary permissions.

Remove Suspicious Apps: If you notice unusual phone behavior (e.g., battery draining quickly, excessive data usage, performance slowdowns) or apps you don't recognize, remove them immediately. Use your phone's app management settings to uninstall suspicious apps.

Antivirus for Mobile: Consider using a reputable antivirus or anti-malware app for your phone. These apps can scan for and detect malicious apps and other mobile threats.

Exploiting Vulnerabilities

(Zero-Day Attacks): Software Flaws

How it Works: Like computer operating systems, phone operating systems (Android and iOS) and apps can have vulnerabilities. Zero-day exploits target vulnerabilities that are unknown to the software vendor and for which no patch is yet available. Attackers can exploit these vulnerabilities to gain unauthorized access to your phone or execute malicious code.

Protection
Regular Updates: Always keep your phone's operating system and apps updated. Manufacturers regularly release security patches to fix known vulnerabilities. Enable automatic updates whenever possible to ensure you receive security patches promptly.
Manufacturer Security Updates: Be aware of your phone manufacturer's update policy. Some older phones may no longer receive security updates, making them more vulnerable. Consider upgrading to a newer phone that receives regular security updates.

Security News and Alerts: Stay informed about security news and alerts related to your phone's operating system and apps. Follow reputable

³³★★★³³

security blogs and news sources to stay updated on emerging threats.

Man-in-the-Middle (MITM) Attacks: Interception on Public Wi-Fi

How it Works: Public Wi-Fi networks, often found in cafes, airports, and hotels, are often insecure. When you connect to an unsecured Wi-Fi network, attackers can position themselves between your phone and the Wi-Fi access point, intercepting your internet traffic (Man-in-the-Middle attack). This allows them to potentially steal sensitive information like login credentials, payment details, or private messages if transmitted over unencrypted connections (HTTP).

Protection
Avoid Public Wi-Fi for Sensitive Activities: Avoid using public Wi-Fi for sensitive activities like online banking, shopping, or accessing confidential information.

Use a VPN: Use a Virtual Private Network (VPN) when using public Wi-Fi. A VPN encrypts your internet connection, creating a secure tunnel for your data, making it much harder for attackers to intercept your traffic even on insecure networks.

HTTPS Everywhere: Ensure websites you visit use HTTPS (Hypertext Transfer Protocol Secure). HTTPS encrypts communication between your browser and the website. Look for the padlock icon in your browser's address bar.

³³★★★³³

Turn Off Wi-Fi When Not in Use: When you are not actively using Wi-Fi, turn it off. This reduces the risk of automatically connecting to rogue Wi-Fi hotspots and minimizes the attack surface.

SIM Card Swapping: Hijacking Your Phone Number

How it Works: SIM card swapping, also known as SIM hijacking, is a social engineering attack targeting your mobile carrier. Attackers trick your mobile carrier into transferring your phone number to a SIM card they control. Once they have your phone number, they can receive your calls and SMS messages, including two-factor authentication (2FA) codes sent to your phone number. This allows them to bypass 2FA and gain access to your online accounts.

Protection
Strong Carrier Account Security: Use strong PINs or passwords for your mobile carrier account. Set up account security questions and enable any security features offered by your carrier to prevent unauthorized SIM swaps.

Two-Factor Authentication Methods: Rely less on SMS-based 2FA. Prefer using authenticator apps (like Google Authenticator, Authy) or hardware security keys for 2FA. These methods are more secure than SMS-based 2FA, as they are not vulnerable to SIM swapping.

³³★★★³³

Carrier Account Monitoring: Monitor your carrier account for any unauthorized changes or activity. Be alert for unexpected service disruptions or SIM card activations.

Awareness of Social Engineering: Be aware of social engineering tactics. Mobile carriers should have procedures to verify your identity before making changes to your account. Be suspicious of unsolicited calls or messages requesting account information or changes.

Bluetooth and NFC Exploits: Wireless Weaknesses

How it Works: Bluetooth and NFC (Near Field Communication) are wireless technologies used for short-range communication. If left enabled, especially in "discoverable" mode for Bluetooth, attackers can potentially exploit vulnerabilities in these protocols to connect to your device, install malware, or access private data. NFC, while requiring closer proximity, can also be exploited in certain scenarios.

Protection
Turn Off When Not in Use: Turn off Bluetooth and NFC when you are not actively using them. Disable "discoverable" mode for Bluetooth.
Avoid Pairing with Unknown Devices: Be cautious about pairing your phone with unknown or untrusted Bluetooth devices. Only pair with devices you recognize and trust.

NFC Awareness: Be mindful of NFC interactions in public places. While NFC requires close proximity, be cautious about unexpected NFC prompts or requests.

Bluetooth Security Updates: Keep your phone's operating system updated to ensure you have the latest Bluetooth security patches.

How to Protect Your Phone: Proactive Security Measures

Protecting your phone requires a proactive and layered security approach. Here are key steps to enhance your phone's security:

1. Use Strong, Unique Passwords

Strong Lock Screen Password/PIN: Use a strong password, PIN, pattern, or biometric authentication (fingerprint, face unlock) to secure your phone's lock screen. A strong password should be a mix of letters, numbers, and symbols.

Unique Account Passwords: Use strong and unique passwords for all your online accounts, especially those accessed via your phone (email, banking, social media). Avoid reusing passwords across multiple accounts.

Password Manager: Consider using a password manager app to generate and store strong, unique passwords securely. Password managers make it easier to manage complex passwords and can auto-fill login credentials, reducing the risk of phishing.

2. Enable Two-Factor Authentication (2FA)

Enable 2FA on Accounts: Enable two-factor authentication (2FA) on all important online accounts that support it, especially email, banking, social media, and cloud storage accounts.

Authenticator Apps Preferred: Use authenticator apps (like Google Authenticator, Authy, Microsoft Authenticator) for 2FA whenever possible. They are more secure than SMS-based 2FA.

Hardware Security Keys: For even stronger security, consider using hardware security keys (like YubiKey, Google Titan Security Key) for accounts that support them.

3. Regular Updates:

OS and App Updates: Keep your phone's operating system (Android or iOS) and all apps up to date. Enable automatic updates whenever possible to ensure you receive security patches promptly. Updates often contain critical security fixes that patch known vulnerabilities.

Security Patches: Pay attention to security patch levels for Android and iOS. Manufacturers often release monthly or quarterly security updates.

4. Antivirus Software:

³³★★★³³

Trusted Antivirus App: Install a trusted antivirus or anti-malware app from a reputable vendor on your phone. Antivirus apps can scan for malicious apps, malware, and other mobile threats.

Real-time Scanning: Choose an antivirus app that provides real-time scanning and protection, monitoring your phone for suspicious activity in the background.

Regular Scans: Run regular manual scans with your antivirus app to check for malware and threats.

5. Backup Data Regularly:

Cloud Backup: Set up automatic cloud backups for your phone's data (photos, contacts, documents, etc.) to services like Google Drive (Android), iCloud (iOS), or third-party cloud backup services.

Local Backup: Consider creating local backups of your phone's data to your computer periodically.

Recovery from Breach: Having regular backups ensures that in case of a breach, malware infection, or data loss, you can restore your data and avoid losing everything.

6. Avoid Rooting or Jailbreaking:

Security Risks: Avoid rooting (Android) or jailbreaking (iOS) your phone. These processes remove built-in security mechanisms and restrictions imposed by the operating system, making your phone significantly more vulnerable to attacks.

Voiding Warranty: Rooting or jailbreaking can also void your phone's warranty and may prevent you from receiving future security updates.

App Store Security: Sticking to the official app stores and avoiding rooting or jailbreaking helps maintain the security integrity of your phone.

Cybercriminal Tool Acquisition for Phone Hacking: Where They Get Their Arsenal

Cyber-criminals obtain the tools and programs needed to hack phones from a variety of sources, ranging from the dark web to legitimate software repositories. Understanding these sources helps in comprehending the accessibility and availability of phone hacking tools.

Dark Web Cybercrime Bazaar

Dark Web Hub: The dark web is a major marketplace for cyber-criminals to buy, sell, and trade hacking tools, malware, and illicit services related to phone hacking.

Marketplace Platforms: Dark web marketplaces (like AlphaBay, Empire Market, or Dream Market, although subject to law enforcement actions) have historically been used to trade hacking tools, stolen credentials, exploits, and mobile malware like RATs, spyware, and phishing kits targeting phones.

33★★★33

Forums and Communities: Cyber-criminals communicate on private forums and dark web communities to share, sell, or exchange malicious programs and tools specifically designed for phone hacking. These may include specialized RATs for mobile devices, exploit kits targeting mobile vulnerabilities, and phishing kits tailored for mobile platforms.

Tool Acquisition Methods

Purchasing Tools: Tools are typically purchased using cryptocurrencies like Bitcoin or Monero for anonymity.

Malware and Exploits: Once purchased from dark web sources, malware or exploit code can be uploaded to the criminal's infrastructure or directly used against victim phones.

Publicly Available Hacking Tools (Repurposed Software): Dual-Use Tools

Ethical Hacking Tools Misused: Some tools designed for ethical hacking and penetration testing are repurposed by cyber-criminals for malicious intent. These tools are often freely available from legitimate sources, making them easily accessible.

33★★★33

Examples of Repurposed Tools

- **Metasploit Framework**: While primarily for penetration testing, `Metasploit` provides exploits and payloads that can be used to compromise phones, particularly in spear-phishing or social engineering attacks. It can be used to create Android payloads and exploit vulnerabilities in mobile applications or systems.
- **Cobalt Strike**: Although commercially designed for red teaming, `Cobalt Strike` can be used by cyber-criminals for post-exploitation tasks on compromised phones (if they can gain initial access), such as privilege escalation, lateral movement (within a phone or connected network), and data exfiltration.
- **Aircrack-ng**: Used for Wi-Fi security testing, criminals can misuse it to crack Wi-Fi passwords, especially when targeting phones connected to vulnerable Wi-Fi networks. Gaining access to a phone's Wi-Fi network can be a step in further compromising the device or intercepting data.

Tool Download Sources

- GitHub and Open Source Repositories: Many hacking tools, including those that can be adapted for phone hacking, are open-source and freely available on platforms like GitHub.

33★★★33

- **Hacker Forums and Websites:**
Cyber-criminals download ready-made
phishing kits, RATs, and malware from
specialized hacker forums and websites,
which may host tools for free or for a fee.
Some of these tools are modified versions
of legitimate penetration testing tools.

Exploit Kits and Remote Access Tools (RATs): Automated Attack Packages

Sold/Shared via Dark Web: Exploit kits and RATs
specifically designed for phone hacking are often
sold or shared through private networks or dark
web channels. These kits automate attacks and
provide remote access to victim devices.

How Exploit Kits Work

• **Mobile Exploit Kits**: Exploit kits designed for
mobile platforms exploit vulnerabilities in mobile
browsers, operating systems (Android, iOS), or
commonly used mobile apps.
• **Drive-by Downloads**: Exploit kits are often
spread through drive-by downloads on
compromised or malicious websites. When a user
visits such a site using their phone browser, the kit
silently exploits vulnerabilities and installs malware.
• **RAT Installation**: Exploit kits may install RATs,
keyloggers, or ransomware on compromised
phones

³³★★★³³

Remote Access Tools (RATs) for Phones

Mobile RATs: RATs designed specifically for mobile operating systems (Android, iOS) are available on hacker forums. Examples include Android RATs like AndroRAT, Dendroid, or commercially available spyware solutions that can be misused.

Full Control over Phone: Once installed on a phone, these RATs give the attacker significant control over the device, including remote monitoring, data theft, and surveillance.

Tool Download Methods

• **Compromised Websites**: Exploit kits are spread through drive-by downloads on compromised or malicious websites.

• **Email Attachments and Links**: Phishing emails are used to trick recipients into downloading RATs or exploit kits as malicious attachments or through links.

Custom-Developed Tools: Bespoke Malware

Coding Skills Required: Some cyber-criminals, particularly those more advanced, develop their own custom malware, RATs, or hacking tools specifically for phone hacking.

Targeted Attacks: Custom tools can be designed to target specific vulnerabilities in a phone's OS, applications, or for specific attack scenarios.

Developing Malware: Cyber-criminals with coding skills (e.g., in Java, C++, Python, or mobile app development languages) create custom malware to target specific vulnerabilities. This includes creating spyware, backdoors, or custom exploits for mobile platforms.

Exploiting Unpatched Vulnerabilities: When zero-day vulnerabilities are discovered, attackers can create custom tools to exploit these flaws before patches are available, enabling them to install malware on devices.

Tool Acquisition

Private Sources: Custom-developed tools are often exchanged or sold privately, through closed forums, dark web marketplaces, or person-to-person transactions. Access to these tools may be limited to trusted parties within the cybercrime community.

Peer-to-Peer (P2P) Sharing and Torrent Networks: Informal Distribution

P2P Networks: Some cyber-criminals use P2P networks and torrent sites to distribute malware or hacking tools, including those for phone hacking.

33★★★33

Sharing via Torrents: Malicious programs like keyloggers, RATs, and exploit kits targeting phones can be distributed through torrent files, which can be downloaded using torrent software. Criminals may disguise malicious programs as legitimate apps, games, or cracked software to trick users into downloading them.

Tool Download Locations

• **Torrent Sites and File-Sharing Platforms**: Tools are uploaded to popular torrent sites or file-sharing platforms, often disguised as harmless software. Users searching for "free apps" or "cracked software" may inadvertently download malicious tools.

Staying Protected: Key Defenses

While cyber-criminals have access to a wide array of tools for phone hacking, individuals and organizations can take effective steps to protect their phones and devices from being compromised:

1. **Official App Stores Only**: Avoid downloading software or apps from untrusted sources. Only install apps from the official Google Play Store (Android) or Apple App Store (iOS).
2. **Keep Software Updated**: Keep your phone's operating system and apps up to date. Install security updates and patches promptly to close known vulnerabilities.

³³★★★³³

3. **Security Software**: Use reputable security software, like antivirus programs, on your phone. Ensure real-time protection is enabled to detect and block malware.

4. **Phishing Awareness**: Be aware of phishing attacks. Never click on suspicious links in emails, text messages, or social media messages. Verify the legitimacy of any communication asking for sensitive information.

5. **Strong Security Settings**: Enable strong passwords, PINs, or biometric authentication on your phone. Use two-factor authentication for online accounts. Encrypt your phone's storage to protect data at rest.

—

Chapter 5 Publicly Available Tools: Ethical Hacking vs.Cybercrime

Publicly available security tools are a double-edged sword. Designed for legitimate purposes like penetration testing and security research, they can also be misused by cyber-criminals to compromise systems, steal data, or deploy malware.

Understanding these tools, their functionalities, ethical uses, and malicious repurposing is crucial for both security professionals and individuals aiming to protect themselves against cyber threats.

Metasploit Framework - Versatile Penetration Testing Toolkit

Description: `Metasploit` is a highly popular open-source framework for penetration testing and exploit development. It's a powerful and versatile toolkit that provides a vast collection of exploits, payloads, and auxiliary modules. `Metasploit` is widely used by security professionals to assess the security posture of systems and networks.

Legitimate Use

Penetration Testing: Security professionals use Metasploit extensively for penetration testing engagements. They use it to identify vulnerabilities in systems and networks, simulate attacks, and

³³★★★³³

assess the effectiveness of security controls. `Metasploit` allows ethical hackers to systematically test defenses and provide recommendations for improvement.

Vulnerability Assessment: `Metasploit`'s vulnerability scanning and exploitation capabilities are used to perform comprehensive vulnerability assessments. Security teams can use it to identify and verify security weaknesses in their infrastructure.

Exploit Development: `Metasploit` provides a platform for security researchers and developers to develop, test, and share new exploits. It facilitates the process of researching vulnerabilities and creating proof-of-concept exploits to demonstrate security flaws.

Malicious Use

Exploiting Unpatched Vulnerabilities: Cyber-criminals misuse `Metasploit` to exploit known vulnerabilities in software, services, and operating systems. They can use it to target systems with unpatched vulnerabilities, particularly those disclosed in CVEs. For example, they might exploit an unpatched Windows SMB vulnerability (like EternalBlue, CVE-2017-0144) to install malware or ransomware.

Post-Exploitation Activities: After compromising a system using `Metasploit` or other means, cyber-criminals leverage `Metasploit`'s Meterpreter payload for extensive post-exploitation activities.

33★★★33

Meterpreter provides a wide range of functionalities, including:

- **Privilege Escalation**: Gaining elevated privileges (admin/root) on the compromised system.
- **Credential Theft**: Using modules like `Mimikatz` (integrated in Meterpreter) to steal credentials.
- **Keylogging**: Recording keystrokes to capture sensitive data.
- **Data Exfiltration**: Stealing files, documents, and credentials from the compromised system.

Lateral Movement: Using Meterpreter to move laterally to other systems within the network.

How Cybercriminals Use It

Vulnerability Identification and Exploitation: Cyber-criminals often begin by using reconnaissance tools like `Nmap` to identify vulnerable systems with open ports and services. They then use `Metasploit` to search for and apply exploits relevant to those vulnerabilities.

Payload Delivery and Control: `Metasploit` is used to craft and deliver payloads (like Meterpreter) to the target system after successful exploitation. Meterpreter provides a persistent and feature-rich shell for controlling the compromised system.

Automated Attack Campaigns: While `Metasploit` can be used for targeted attacks, cyber-criminals can also use it to automate parts of their attack campaigns, scanning for vulnerabilities, launching exploits, and deploying payloads across multiple systems.

2. Cobalt Strike: Advanced Red Teaming and Adversary Simulation Tool

Description: `Cobalt Strike` is a commercial tool specifically designed for penetration testing and adversary simulation. It's a sophisticated platform used for red teaming operations, simulating advanced persistent threats (APTs), and assessing organizational defenses against sophisticated cyber-attacks.

Legitimate Use

Red Teaming Exercises: Security teams use `Cobalt Strike` to conduct realistic red teaming exercises, simulating advanced cyber-attacks to evaluate an organization's detection and response capabilities. Red teams mimic the tactics, techniques, and procedures (TTPs) of real-world adversaries.

Adversary Simulation: `Cobalt Strike` helps security teams simulate the behavior of advanced persistent threats (APTs). It allows them to emulate covert command-and-control (C2) communication, lateral movement within networks, and data exfiltration techniques used by APT groups. This helps organizations understand their vulnerabilities against advanced attackers.

33★★★33

Security Control Validation: `Cobalt Strike` is used to validate the effectiveness of security controls, such as intrusion detection systems (IDS), intrusion prevention systems (IPS), endpoint detection and response (EDR) solutions, and security information and event management (SIEM) systems. By simulating attacks, organizations can test whether their security controls are working as intended.

Malicious Use

Command-and-Control (C2) Infrastructure: Cyber-criminals leverage `Cobalt Strike`'s powerful command-and-control (C2) capabilities to establish covert communication channels with infected systems. They use the Beacon payload to create persistent and stealthy C2 infrastructure, enabling long-term control over compromised networks.

Beacon Payload for Remote Access: The `Cobalt Strike` Beacon payload is a key component misused by cyber-criminals. Once deployed on a compromised system, Beacon maintains persistence, receives commands from the C2 server, and establishes encrypted communication channels, allowing attackers to control infected devices and exfiltrate data remotely.

Lateral Movement and Privilege Escalation: `Cobalt Strike`'s lateral movement and privilege escalation features are abused by cyber-criminals to move across networks and gain access to sensitive systems. They mimic the tactics used by advanced cyber-criminal groups to expand their reach within a compromised network.

How Cybercriminals Use It
Post-Exploitation Command and Control: After gaining initial access to a system (e.g., through phishing or exploiting a vulnerability), cyber-criminals deploy `Cobalt Strike`'s Beacon payload. They use Beacon to establish a persistent C2 connection, allowing them to control the infected device remotely.

Lateral Movement and Network Domination: `Cobalt Strike`'s lateral movement capabilities are used to spread throughout a target network, moving from the initially compromised system to other machines. They aim to gain control over critical systems and domain controllers.

Data Theft and Ransomware Deployment: Once they have established broad network access, cyber-criminals use `Cobalt Strike` for data exfiltration and deploying ransomware payloads across the network, often aiming for maximum impact and disruption.

3. Aircrack-ng: Wi-Fi Security Auditing and Cracking Tool

Description: `Aircrack-ng` is a comprehensive suite of tools for wireless network auditing and security testing. It's primarily designed for Wi-Fi security assessments and supports various platforms (Linux, Windows, macOS). `Aircrack-ng`

33★★★33

allows users to test the security of wireless networks, including cracking WEP and WPA-PSK encryption.

Legitimate Use

Wi-Fi Security Audits: Security professionals use `Aircrack-ng` to assess the security of wireless networks. They check for weak encryption protocols (like WEP), poor configurations, and vulnerabilities that could allow unauthorized access to Wi-Fi networks.

Penetration Testing of Wireless Networks: `Aircrack-ng` is a key tool in penetration testing wireless networks. It helps assess whether a Wi-Fi network is vulnerable to attacks like WEP cracking, WPA/WPA2 brute-forcing, or man-in-the-middle attacks.

Network Security Training: `Aircrack-ng` is often used in cybersecurity training and education to demonstrate Wi-Fi security vulnerabilities and teach students about wireless network security principles and best practices.

Malicious Use

Cracking Wi-Fi Passwords: Cyber-criminals misuse `Aircrack-ng` to break into poorly secured wireless networks by cracking WEP or WPA encryption keys. Once inside a Wi-Fi network, they can intercept traffic, launch man-in-the-middle (MITM) attacks, or gain access to devices connected to the network.

³³★★★³³

Packet Sniffing and Data Interception:
`Aircrack-ng` can capture wireless packets transmitted over the air. Cyber-criminals use this to capture packets and collect sensitive data from unsuspecting victims on unprotected Wi-Fi networks, potentially intercepting passwords, session tokens, or other confidential information.

Wi-Fi Network Disruption: `Aircrack-ng` includes tools for deauthentication attacks, allowing attackers to disconnect users from Wi-Fi networks. This can be used for denial-of-service (DoS) attacks or as a prelude to other attacks, forcing users to reconnect to a rogue access point controlled by the attacker.

How Cybercriminals Use It

Wi-Fi Password Cracking for Network Access:
Cyber-criminals use `Aircrack-ng` to target Wi-Fi networks with weak or default passwords. They capture Wi-Fi traffic, perform brute-force attacks to recover WEP or WPA encryption keys, and gain unauthorized access to the Wi-Fi network.

Man-in-the-Middle Attacks on Wi-Fi Networks:
Once inside a Wi-Fi network, attackers can use `Aircrack-ng` in conjunction with other tools to launch man-in-the-middle (MITM) attacks. They can intercept traffic between devices on the Wi-Fi network and the internet, potentially stealing credentials or injecting malicious content.

Wi-Fi Network Spoofing (Evil Twin Attacks):
`Aircrack-ng` can be used in setting up rogue Wi-Fi access points (Evil Twin attacks). Attackers create

a fake Wi-Fi network with the same name as a legitimate one to trick users into connecting to their malicious network, allowing them to intercept traffic and launch further attacks.

4. `Nmap (Network Mapper): Network Discovery and Vulnerability Scanning

Description: `Nmap` is a widely used network scanning tool for network discovery, security auditing, and vulnerability scanning. It provides network administrators and security professionals with capabilities to map out network topologies, discover open ports, services, and potential vulnerabilities on target systems.

Legitimate Use

Network Inventory and Mapping: Security professionals use `Nmap` to create an inventory of devices and services on their networks. It helps map network topologies, identify connected systems, and understand network infrastructure.

Vulnerability Scanning and Assessment: `Nmap` is used for vulnerability scanning, identifying open ports and running services on systems, which can indicate potential security vulnerabilities. Security teams use `Nmap` to identify weaknesses in their systems and prioritize patching efforts.

Compliance Auditing: `Nmap` helps organizations ensure compliance with security policies and standards. It can be used to verify that only authorized ports and services are open on systems, and that security configurations are in line with organizational policies.

Troubleshooting Network Issues: Network administrators use `Nmap` to troubleshoot network connectivity problems. It can help identify network bottlenecks, diagnose service outages, and verify network configurations.

Malicious Use

Reconnaissance and Target Profiling: Cyber-criminals use `Nmap` extensively for reconnaissance. They scan target networks to identify live hosts, open ports, and running services. This information allows them to profile their targets, understand their network infrastructure, and identify potential attack vectors.

Vulnerability Discovery for Exploitation: Attackers use `Nmap` to discover vulnerable services and systems within a target network. Identifying open ports and services helps them pinpoint potential entry points and targets for exploitation. They look for services known to have vulnerabilities, like outdated web servers, databases, or network protocols.

Service Enumeration and Attack Surface Mapping: `Nmap` allows attackers to enumerate the services running on target systems. This helps them understand the attack surface of the network, identify potential vulnerabilities in specific services

³³★★★³³

(e.g., FTP, SSH, HTTP), and plan their attacks accordingly.

How Cybercriminals Use It

Initial Reconnaissance of Target Networks: Cyber-criminals typically start their attacks by using `Nmap` to perform network scans of their target organizations or individuals. They map out the network, identify systems and services that are accessible from the internet or within internal networks.

Vulnerability Assessment and Exploitation Planning: `Nmap`' scan results are used to assess the vulnerability landscape of the target. Attackers look for systems with open ports, running outdated services, or exhibiting characteristics of known vulnerabilities. This information guides their exploit selection and attack planning.

Identifying Entry Points and Targets: `Nmap` helps attackers identify potential entry points into a network. They look for exposed services that might be vulnerable to exploitation, such as web servers, VPN gateways, or remote access services. They also identify key target systems within the network, like servers, databases, or critical workstations.

5. Hydra (THC-Hydra): Password Cracking and Brute-Force Tool

Description: `Hydra` (THC-Hydra) is a powerful password-cracking tool used for brute-forcing authentication credentials against various network protocols. It supports a wide range of protocols, including HTTP, FTP, SSH, RDP, and many others. `Hydra` is designed to test password strength and the resilience of authentication mechanisms.

Legitimate Use

Password Audits and Strength Testing: IT professionals use `Hydra` to perform password audits and test the strength of passwords used within their organizations. They can use it to identify weak or easily guessable passwords and enforce stronger password policies.

Penetration Testing of Authentication Systems: `Hydra` is a valuable tool during penetration tests to assess the robustness of login systems. Security testers use it to try various password combinations against login forms and authentication services to identify vulnerabilities in password security.

Credential Recovery (Ethical Scenarios): In some ethical scenarios (e.g., recovering forgotten passwords with permission), `Hydra` can be used to attempt password recovery using dictionary attacks or known password patterns.

Malicious Use

Brute-Force Attacks on Login Forms: Cyber-criminals misuse `Hydra` to launch brute-force attacks against login forms of websites, applications, and network services. They try numerous password combinations from dictionaries or generated lists to crack weak passwords and gain unauthorized access to accounts.

Credential Stuffing Attacks: `Hydra` can be used in credential stuffing attacks. Attackers use lists of stolen usernames and passwords (often obtained from data breaches) and configure `Hydra` to perform mass login attempts on various sites and services. If users have reused the same passwords across multiple platforms, `Hydra` can successfully gain access to accounts.

Automated Password Cracking: `Hydra` automates the process of password cracking. Cyber-criminals can configure it to run for extended periods, attempting thousands or millions of password combinations, increasing their chances of cracking weak passwords.

How Cybercriminals Use It

Automated Password Cracking for Account Access: Cyber-criminals use `Hydra` to automate password cracking against various online accounts, systems, and services. They target login pages, SSH servers, FTP servers, RDP services, and other authentication points.

Brute-Forcing Weak Passwords: `Hydra` is effective against systems or accounts that use weak passwords. Attackers often use dictionary attacks (trying common passwords from wordlists) or hybrid attacks (combining dictionary words with numbers and symbols) to crack passwords.

33★★★33

Credential Stuffing for Account Takeover: As mentioned, `Hydra` is used for credential stuffing. Attackers feed `Hydra` with lists of stolen usernames and passwords from data breaches and use it to attempt login attempts across multiple platforms. If users have reused passwords, attackers can gain access to multiple accounts using this technique.

6. Burp Suite: Web Application Security Testing and Attack Tool

Description: `Burp Suite` is a popular and comprehensive web application security testing toolkit. It's widely used by security professionals to perform intercepting proxy, vulnerability scanning, and security testing of web applications. `Burp Suite` is a powerful platform for identifying security weaknesses in web apps.

Legitimate Use

Web Application Penetration Testing: Security professionals extensively use `Burp Suite` for web application penetration testing. It provides tools to identify vulnerabilities like cross-site scripting (XSS), SQL injection, command injection, authentication bypasses, and other common web application flaws.

Vulnerability Scanning: `Burp Suite`'s vulnerability scanner automates the process of finding common web application vulnerabilities. It can scan websites and web applications for a wide range of security weaknesses, helping security teams quickly identify potential issues.

Manual and Automated Security Testing: `Burp Suite` supports both manual and automated security testing workflows. Security testers can manually explore web applications, intercept and modify requests, and use automated scanners to find vulnerabilities efficiently.

Security Training and Education: `Burp Suite` is often used in cybersecurity training and education to teach web application security testing techniques and demonstrate web vulnerabilities.

Malicious Use

Web Application Attacks and Exploitation: Cyber-criminals misuse `Burp Suite` to launch web application attacks. They use its intercepting proxy to intercept and manipulate web traffic, allowing them to exploit vulnerabilities like SQL injection, cross-site scripting (XSS), and other web app flaws.

Data Exfiltration and Manipulation: `Burp Suite`'s capabilities to intercept and modify web traffic can be abused to exfiltrate data from compromised web applications or servers. Attackers can manipulate web requests and responses to extract sensitive information or modify application behavior for malicious purposes.

Automated Web Application Attacks: `Burp Suite`'s Intruder tool can be used to automate brute-force attacks, parameter manipulation attacks, and other types of automated attacks against web applications. Cyber-criminals can use Intruder to launch large-scale attacks to find vulnerabilities or gain unauthorized access.

How Cybercriminals Use It

Intercepting Web Traffic for Vulnerability Discovery: Cyber-criminals use `Burp Suite`'s intercepting proxy to intercept web traffic between a user's browser and a web server. They analyze the intercepted requests and responses to identify potential vulnerabilities in the web application.

Manual Vulnerability Exploitation: `Burp Suite` allows attackers to manually exploit web vulnerabilities. For example, they can use the Repeater tool to send modified requests to test for SQL injection vulnerabilities or XSS flaws. They can manipulate parameters, inject malicious payloads, and observe the application's responses to confirm and exploit vulnerabilities.

Automated Attack Automation with Intruder: `Burp Suite`'s Intruder tool is used to automate various types of web application attacks. Attackers can use Intruder for brute-forcing login forms, performing parameter fuzzing to find hidden parameters or vulnerabilities, or launching automated SQL injection attacks.

Final Thoughts: Responsible Use and Defense

33★★★33

While these publicly available tools are essential for cybersecurity professionals and ethical hackers, their misuse by cyber-criminals can lead to significant harm. Understanding how these tools function and how they are used in both ethical and unethical contexts is crucial for both security professionals and the public.

For Security Professionals: Mastering these tools and understanding their malicious applications is essential for effective defense. Security professionals must use these tools ethically to protect systems and networks, conduct vulnerability assessments, and simulate attacks to improve security posture.

For the Public: Awareness of these tools and the types of attacks they enable helps individuals and organizations understand the threats they face. Implementing strong security practices, keeping software updated, and being vigilant against phishing and social engineering attacks are crucial steps in mitigating risks associated with these powerful tools.

Chapter 6 Setting Up Malicious Websites

The Digital Lure

Setting up malicious websites is a critical step in many cyber-criminal operations. These websites act as digital lures, designed to host malware, deliver phishing attacks, or exploit vulnerabilities in visitors' browsers or devices. Understanding how cyber-criminals set up and run these malicious websites is crucial for defense. This chapter breaks down the process, focusing on the tools and techniques involved.

Domain Registration and Hosting: Establishing the Malicious Base

The first step is to establish a web presence for the malicious operation, which involves registering a domain name and securing web hosting.

Choosing a Deceptive Domain Name:
Cyber-criminals carefully choose domain names that resemble legitimate websites to deceive visitors. This is a core tactic in phishing and malware distribution.

- *Typosquatting*: They register domain names that are very similar to popular websites, but with slight typos (e.g., "amaz0n.com" instead of "amazon.com")

³³★★★³³

Users might mistyped URLs and land on the malicious site.

- **Similar-Looking Domains**: They use domain names that look visually similar to legitimate ones, using different top-level domains (TLDs) or character substitutions.

- **Expired SSL Certificates Exploitation**: Registering domains with expired SSL certificates can make the site appear less secure, but in some cases, attackers may exploit this to further social engineering attacks, claiming the site is legitimate but has a temporary certificate issue.

Anonymous Registration: To hide their identity and avoid being traced back to the malicious website, cyber-criminals use anonymous domain registration services.

WHOIS Privacy Protection: They utilize WHOIS privacy protection services offered by domain registrars. These services replace the registrant's personal information in the public WHOIS database with the registrar's contact details, masking the true owner.

Fake Identities: In some cases, attackers use completely fake identities when registering domains, providing false names, addresses, and contact information. This makes it more difficult for investigators to identify the real owner.

33★★★33

Hosting the Website: Finding a Safe Haven

Compromised Web Hosts: A common and cost-effective approach is to use compromised servers or vulnerable web hosting services.

Exploiting Vulnerabilities: Attackers scan for vulnerable web servers or hosting accounts. Once they find a vulnerable system, they exploit it to gain unauthorized access and host their malicious website on the compromised server. This is often done without the knowledge or consent of the hosting provider or legitimate website owner.

Stolen Hosting Accounts: Cyber-criminals may also steal or purchase stolen web hosting accounts from compromised providers or on dark web marketplaces.

Bulletproof Hosting: Safe Harbor for Cybercrime: For more advanced and resilient malicious operations, cyber-criminals turn to bulletproof hosting providers for a few reasons:

- **Ignoring Law Enforcement**: Bulletproof hosting providers are services that are designed to protect cyber-criminals from law enforcement and takedown requests. They operate with a "no questions asked" approach and often ignore or refuse to cooperate with takedown requests from authorities.
- **Located in Lax Jurisdictions**: Bulletproof hosting providers are often located in countries with lax internet regulations,

³³★★★³³

where law enforcement cooperation is limited or non-existent.

- **Anonymity and Resilience**: Bulletproof hosting provides anonymity to cyber-criminals and makes their malicious websites more resilient to takedown attempts.

Cloud Hosting Services (Abuse): Hiding in the Crowd: Ironically, cyber-criminals sometimes abuse legitimate cloud service providers like Amazon Web Services (AWS) or Microsoft Azure to host malicious websites.

Stolen or Fake Accounts: They may use stolen or fake accounts to sign up for cloud hosting services. Cloud providers often have automated signup processes, making it easier to create accounts with minimal verification.

Bypassing Detection (Initially): Initially, hosting malicious websites on cloud providers might help bypass detection, as traffic to well-known cloud services may appear legitimate. However, cloud providers have security measures in place and will eventually shut down accounts and websites hosting malicious content if detected.

2. Website Construction: Building the Digital Trap

Once the domain and hosting are secured, the malicious site itself is constructed. The design and functionality of the site depend on the attacker's goals, ranging from simple phishing pages to sophisticated sites designed to exploit browser vulnerabilities.

Phishing Pages: Mimicking Legitimate Sites

Copying Legitimate Websites (Cloning): To maximize deception, cyber-criminals meticulously replicate legitimate websites. They clone the visual appearance, layout, branding, and content of target websites, making the fake pages look almost indistinguishable from the real ones.

Tools for Cloning: Tools like `Social Engineering Toolkit (SET)` and `HTTrack Website Copier` can automate the process of cloning websites, making it easier and faster to create convincing phishing pages.

Fake Forms and Credential Harvesting: The core purpose of phishing pages is to capture user input, particularly login credentials and sensitive information.

- **Fake Login Forms**: Phishing pages contain fake forms that mimic login forms of legitimate services (banking portals, email login pages, e-commerce sites). These forms are designed to capture usernames and passwords when users enter them, sending the captured credentials to the attacker's server.

³³★★★³³

- **Fake Payment Forms:** For financial phishing, pages may include fake payment forms designed to steal credit card details, bank account information, or other financial data.

JavaScript Obfuscation: Hiding Malicious Code: To evade detection by security tools and make analysis more difficult, attackers often obfuscate malicious JavaScript code embedded in phishing pages.

Code Obfuscation Techniques: Techniques like string encoding, variable renaming, control flow obfuscation, and tools like `JSFuck` are used to make JavaScript code unreadable and harder to analyze. This is done to hide the malicious functionality, such as data theft scripts, credential exfiltration code, or triggers for malicious payloads.

Malware Distribution Sites: Silent Infection Vectors

Drive-by Downloads: Automatic Malware Delivery: Some malicious websites are designed to silently download malware onto visitors' devices without requiring user interaction. This is achieved through drive-by download techniques.

Malvertising: Malicious advertisements (malvertising) are injected into legitimate advertising networks. When users visit websites displaying these malicious ads, they can be redirected to malware distribution sites or trigger drive-by downloads directly.

Exploiting Browser Vulnerabilities: Malicious websites can exploit vulnerabilities in web browsers (like Chrome, Firefox, Internet Explorer) or browser plugins (like Flash, Java, PDF readers). By hosting specially crafted content, they can trigger vulnerabilities that lead to automatic malware downloads when a user visits the site.

JavaScript, Flash, and PDF Exploits: Attackers use JavaScript, Flash (increasingly less relevant as Flash is phased out), and PDF exploits to trigger vulnerabilities and deliver malware.

Exploit Kits: Automated Vulnerability Scanning and Exploitation: Exploit kits are pre-packaged sets of malicious tools designed to automate the process of scanning visitors' browsers and devices for vulnerabilities and then exploiting those vulnerabilities to deliver malware.

Automated Vulnerability Scanning: When a user visits a malicious site hosting an exploit kit, the Kit automatically scans the visitor's browser, browser plugins, and operating system for known vulnerabilities.

Exploiting Weaknesses: If vulnerabilities are found (unpatched Flash or Java vulnerabilities), the exploit kit selects and launches the appropriate exploit code to take advantage of those weaknesses.

- **Malware Delivery**: Once exploitation is successful, the exploit kit delivers and installs malware onto the victim's system, often without any user interaction.
  - **Popular Exploit Kits (Past and Present):** Well-known exploit kits include RIG, Angler, Neutrino, and Blackhole (although Black Hole is largely defunct due to law enforcement actions)

Fake Software Updates: Social Engineering Trick for Malware Installation: A common social engineering trick is to display fake software update prompts on malicious websites.

Mimicking Legitimate Updates: These prompts are designed to look like legitimate update notifications for software like Adobe Flash, Java, Windows, or antivirus programs.

Malware Disguised as Updates: When a user clicks on the fake "update" button, they are actually tricked into downloading and installing malware instead of a legitimate software update. The malware payload is often disguised as an update installer file.

Web Shells and Backdoors: Remote Server Control

Web Shells for Server Access: Attackers may place web shells on compromised web servers to gain remote access and control over the server.

Script-Based Backdoors: A web shell is a script (often written in PHP, ASP, Python, or other web scripting languages) that is uploaded to a web server. Once in place, the attacker can access and control the server through a web browser by sending commands to the web shell.

Remote Server Management: Web shells provide a web-based interface for attackers to manage the compromised server remotely. They can execute system commands, browse files, upload and download files, modify configurations, and perform other administrative tasks on the server through the web shell interface.

Malicious Actions via Web Shells: Web shells are used to perform a variety of malicious actions, including:

Downloading More Malware: Downloading and installing additional malware onto the server and potentially onto connected systems.

Data Theft from Server: Stealing data stored on the server, including databases, configuration files, and sensitive documents.

Launching Attacks on Other Sites: Using the compromised server as a launching point for attacks on other websites or networks, leveraging its resources and network connectivity.

Backdoor Access for Persistence: Once a web shell or backdoor is set up, attackers configure the site to provide ongoing access, ensuring persistence even if one attack vector is discovered or patched.

Persistent Remote Access: Backdoors ensure that even if the initial vulnerability used to compromise the server is patched or if other access methods are blocked, the attacker can still maintain control and re-enter the system through the backdoor.

3. Drive-by Downloads and Exploit Chains: Automated Infection

For attackers aiming to install malware without direct user interaction, drive-by downloads and exploit chains are powerful techniques.

Exploit Kits: Automated Exploit Delivery Systems

What Exploit Kits Do: Exploit kits are pre-packaged sets of malicious tools designed to automate the process of exploiting vulnerabilities. They are essentially "attack-as-a-service" platforms for cyber-criminals.

Automated Scanning and Exploitation: When a user visits a malicious site hosting an exploit kit, the kit automatically scans the visitor's browser, browser plugins, and operating system for known vulnerabilities.

Vulnerability Exploitation Chain: Exploit kits contain a collection of exploits targeting various vulnerabilities. They select and launch the appropriate exploit based on the vulnerabilities detected on the visitor's system. This creates an "exploit chain" – a sequence of exploits used to compromise a target.

Malware Delivery and Installation: Upon successful exploitation, the exploit kit delivers and installs a malware payload onto the victim's system. The payload can be ransomware, Trojans, spyware, or other types of malware, depending on the attacker's objective.

Popular Exploit Kits (Examples)

RIG Exploit Kit: A widely used and actively developed exploit kit known for its adaptability and frequent updates.

Angler Exploit Kit (Inactive): Angler was once a highly sophisticated and prevalent exploit kit, known for its advanced evasion techniques. However, it became largely inactive after law enforcement actions.

Neutrino Exploit Kit (Inactive): Neutrino was another popular exploit kit, also now largely inactive.

Blackhole Exploit Kit (Defunct): Blackhole was a notorious exploit kit, but it was shut down due to law enforcement efforts.

Common Vulnerabilities Targeted by Exploit Kits

Java Vulnerabilities (e.g., CVE-2016-0603): Exploiting vulnerabilities in the Java Runtime

33★★★33

Environment (JRE) was a common tactic, as Java was widely used as a browser plugin.

Flash Vulnerabilities (e.g., CVE-2015-0313): Adobe Flash Player was another frequent target due to its widespread use and history of security flaws.

Browser Vulnerabilities (e.g., IE, Chrome Bugs): Exploiting vulnerabilities in web browsers themselves (like Internet Explorer, Chrome, Firefox) is a core function of exploit kits.

PDF Reader Vulnerabilities (e.g., CVE-2017-3021): Vulnerabilities in PDF readers (like Adobe Acrobat Reader) were also targeted to deliver malware through malicious PDF files.

Drive-by Downloads: Passive Malware Infections

How Drive-by Downloads Work: In a drive-by download attack, malware is automatically downloaded to a user's system simply by visiting a malicious website, without requiring any explicit action from the user (like clicking a download button). The infection happens "drive-by," as the user passively visits the site.

Exploiting Outdated Software: Drive-by downloads typically exploit outdated or unpatched software on the user's system, such as outdated web browsers, browser plugins (like Flash or Java), or operating system vulnerabilities.

Silent and Unintentional Infection: Users may not even realize that malware is being downloaded in the background when they visit a compromised site, making drive-by downloads stealthy and effective.

Types of Malware Delivered via Drive-by Downloads

Ransomware (Locky, Cerber): Ransomware can be delivered via drive-by downloads, encrypting files upon infection and demanding ransom.

Trojans for Remote Access: Trojans that provide remote access to the attacker (RATs) can be installed through drive-by downloads, allowing for long-term control.

Spyware for Data Theft: Spyware designed to steal sensitive information (login credentials, financial data, personal information) can be deployed via drive-by downloads.

Adware and Cryptojackers: Less overtly malicious malware like adware (displaying unwanted advertisements) or cryptojackers (secretly mining cryptocurrency using victim's resources) can also be distributed through drive-by downloads.

33★★★33

4. Hosting Malicious Content: Delivering the Payload

Once the malicious website is live and functioning, cyber-criminals host various types of malicious content, depending on their attack goals.

Malware Hosting: Distributing Malicious Software

Dropper Files for Secondary Malware:
Cyber-criminals host "dropper" files on their malicious websites. Droppers are small, seemingly innocuous files designed to download and install additional, more complex malware onto the victim's system.

Silent Installation: Droppers often perform their malicious actions silently in the background, without alerting the user.

Secondary Malware Delivery: They are used to download and install secondary malware payloads, such as keyloggers, remote access Trojans (RATs), ransomware, or other malicious software. Droppers act as the initial infection vector, setting the stage for more damaging malware.

Cryptojacking Scripts: Mining Cryptocurrency in the Browser: Some malicious websites host cryptojacking scripts, which hijack visitors' systems to mine cryptocurrency without their knowledge or consent.

Browser-Based Mining: These scripts are typically written in JavaScript and run within the visitor's web browser when they visit the malicious site.

Resource Hijacking: Cryptojacking scripts use the visitor's CPU power and system resources to mine cryptocurrencies (often Monero). This can slow down the user's system and consume excessive resources.

Silent Operation: Cryptojacking scripts often run silently in the background, without any visible indication to the user that their system is being used for cryptocurrency mining.

Phishing Hosting: Luring Victims for Credential Theft

Fake Login Pages for Credential Capture: Malicious websites designed for phishing host fake login pages for popular online services.

- **Mimicking Login Interfaces**: These pages are designed to mimic the login pages of popular services like email providers (Gmail, Outlook), banking websites, social media platforms (Facebook, Twitter), e-commerce sites (Amazon, eBay), or corporate portals.

- **Username and Password Theft**: The primary goal is to capture usernames and passwords when users enter them into the fake login forms. The captured credentials are then sent to the attacker.

³³★★★³³

Email Phishing Links: Driving Traffic to Malicious Sites: Email phishing campaigns are commonly used to drive traffic to malicious websites.

- **Deceptive Emails**: Cyber-criminals send well-crafted phishing emails that are designed to trick recipients into clicking on links.

- **Legitimate Impersonation**: These emails often impersonate legitimate companies, services, or organizations, making them appear trustworthy.

- **Urgent or Enticing Messages**: Phishing emails often use urgent or enticing language to pressure recipients into clicking the links, such as warnings about account security, notifications about unpaid bills, or offers of prizes or rewards.

- **Links to Phishing Sites**: The links embedded in phishing emails lead to the malicious websites hosting fake login pages or malware distribution sites. When users click on these links, they are directed to the attacker's malicious infrastructure.

5. Evasion and Obfuscation: Hiding from Detection

Cyber-criminals take steps to evade detection by security tools and block takedown efforts. Evasion and obfuscation techniques are crucial for maintaining the longevity of malicious websites.

Content Obfuscation: Making Malicious Code Unreadable

JavaScript Obfuscation: Malicious JavaScript code embedded in websites, particularly in phishing pages or exploit kits, is often obfuscated.

Code Transformation: Obfuscation techniques transform the code, making it harder for security analysts and automated tools to understand its functionality.

Evasion of Security Scanners: Obfuscation helps evade detection by web security scanners, antivirus programs, and other security tools that analyze website code for malicious patterns.

Techniques: Common JavaScript obfuscation techniques include

- **String Encoding**: Encoding strings to hide readable text.

- **Variable Renaming**: Renaming variables to meaningless or random names.

- **Control Flow Obfuscation**: Altering the control flow of the code to make it less linear and harder to follow.

- **Code Packing**: Compressing and encoding code into a smaller, less readable form.

HTML/CSS Obfuscation: In addition to JavaScript, cyber-criminals may also obfuscate HTML or CSS code to make it harder for security software to detect malicious elements within the website's structure and presentation.

Anti-Detection Measures: Fooling Security Systems

User-Agent Spoofing: Differentiating Visitors. To prevent being flagged by security services, attackers may modify the site's behavior based on the visitor's user-agent string (information sent by the browser identifying itself).

Different Content for Scanners vs. Victims: They may display different content to security scanners, web crawlers, or researchers compared to what is shown to actual potential victims.

Detection Evasion: By detecting user-agent patterns associated with security tools, they can serve benign content to scanners while serving malicious content only to regular users, effectively evading automated detection.

Geo-blocking: Targeting Specific Regions: Some malicious sites implement geo-blocking, restricting access based on the visitor's geographic location.

Targeted Attacks: They may only target users from specific countries or regions where they believe their victims are most likely to be located.
Reduced Exposure: Geo-blocking can also be used to block visitors from countries known for cybersecurity research or law enforcement, reducing exposure and the likelihood of detection and takedown efforts.

6. Maintenance and Monetization: Keeping the Scheme Running

Once the malicious site is live and functioning, cyber-criminals engage in maintenance activities and monetize their operation.

Monetizing the Site

Converting Malice into Money

Credential Harvesting: Stolen credentials (usernames, passwords, credit card information) are a primary source of monetization.

Dark Web Sales: Captured credentials are sold on underground forums or dark web marketplaces to other cyber-criminals.
Account Takeover: Attackers may also directly use stolen credentials for account takeover, accessing victims' accounts for financial fraud, identity theft, or further malicious activities.

³³★★★³³

Ransomware Delivery: Malicious websites can be used to deliver ransomware.

- **Initial Infection Vector**: The website can be the initial infection point, delivering ransomware directly through drive-by downloads or exploit kits.
- **Secondary Payload Distribution**: In some cases, the website might initially deliver a dropper or loader malware, which then downloads and installs ransomware as a secondary payload.

Ad Fraud or Cryptojacking (Passive Revenue): Less direct monetization methods include ad fraud and cryptojacking.

- **Ad Fraud**: Malicious websites can redirect visitors to third-party ad networks, generating revenue for the attackers through fraudulent ad impressions or clicks.
- **Cryptojacking**: As mentioned, cryptojacking scripts can be hosted on malicious sites to silently mine cryptocurrency using visitors' system resources, generating passive revenue for the attackers.

Maintaining Persistence: Long-Term Operation

Backdoor Access for Long-Term Control: Attackers install web shells or other backdoors on compromised servers to maintain long-term access.

³³★★★³³

Ongoing Control: Backdoors ensure that even if vulnerabilities are patched or security measures are updated, the attacker retains persistent control over the server.

Ongoing Attacks: Persistent access allows attackers to launch ongoing attacks, deliver new malware, steal data continuously, or use the compromised server for future malicious operations.

Updating Malware and Phishing Tools: Cyber-criminals periodically update the malware, phishing tools, and exploit kits hosted on their malicious websites.

Improved Efficacy: Updates aim to improve the efficacy of their attacks, enhance evasion capabilities, and bypass newly implemented detection systems.

Bypass Detection: Updating tools is essential to stay ahead of security software and maintain the effectiveness of the malicious website over time.

Defensive Measures Against Malicious Websites: Building Your Digital Fort

Protecting against malicious websites requires a multi-faceted approach, combining individual vigilance and organizational security measures.

33★★★33

Keep Software Up to Date: Regularly update your operating system, web browsers, browser plugins (though plugins should be minimized), and all software applications. Patches often fix known vulnerabilities exploited by malicious websites.

Use Robust Web Filtering Tools: Implement web filtering tools (e.g., DNS filtering, URL filtering) at both individual and organizational levels. These tools block access to known malicious websites and categories of risky sites, reducing the chance of accidental visits to malicious domains.

Endpoint Security Tools: Deploy strong endpoint security tools, such as antivirus software, anti-malware programs, and endpoint detection and response (EDR) solutions, on all devices. These tools can detect malware infections, block drive-by downloads, and identify phishing attempts.

- **Two-Factor Authentication (2FA):** Enable two-factor authentication (2FA) on important online accounts, especially those accessed through web browsers. 2FA adds an extra layer of security, making it harder for attackers to compromise accounts even if they steal login credentials through phishing websites.
- **User Education and Awareness**: Educate users about the risks of malicious websites, phishing attacks, and drive-by downloads. Train them to recognize phishing emails, suspicious links, and fake update prompts. Emphasize the importance of verifying website legitimacy and avoiding untrusted sources.

₃₃★★★₃₃

By understanding how cyber-criminals set up and use malicious websites, both individuals and organizations can better prepare their systems, educate their users, and implement effective defensive measures to avoid falling victim to these types of attacks.

Chapter 7 Targeting Small Businesses

Exploiting Open Wi-Fi and Limited Defenses

Small businesses, particularly restaurants, often have limited cybersecurity resources and may operate with open Wi-Fi networks for customer convenience. This combination makes them attractive targets for cyber-criminals. This chapter explores the common tactics cyber-criminals might employ against a small restaurant business, especially those with open Wi-Fi.

Man-in-the-Middle (MITM) Attack: Intercepting Wi-Fi Traffic

Open Wi-Fi networks are inherently insecure and provide a prime environment for Man-in-the-Middle (MITM) attacks. Cyber-criminals can easily position themselves between users (restaurant customers or employees) and the Wi-Fi router, intercepting and potentially manipulating all network traffic.

How MITM Attacks Work on Open Wi-Fi

Deauthentication Attack

³³★★★³³

(Forcing Reconnection): Attackers might initiate a deauthentication attack to disrupt the legitimate Wi-Fi network temporarily.

• **Deauthentication Packets**: They send deauthentication packets to all connected devices, forcing them to disconnect from the legitimate Wi-Fi access point.

• **Automatic Reconnection**: When devices attempt to reconnect to the Wi-Fi, they might automatically connect to the attacker's rogue access point if it has a stronger signal or is presented as the more readily available option.

Rogue Access Point (Evil Twin): Attackers set up a rogue Wi-Fi access point (an "Evil Twin") that mimics the legitimate restaurant's Wi-Fi network.

• **SSID Spoofing**: They configure their rogue access point to use the same SSID (network name) as the restaurant's Wi-Fi. If the restaurant uses an open Wi-Fi without a password, the rogue AP will also be open and easily joinable.

• **Stronger Signal or Deception**: The rogue AP might have a stronger Wi-Fi signal or be strategically placed to attract connections. Attackers might also use social engineering to trick users into connecting to their rogue network.

Packet Sniffing and Traffic Interception: Once devices connect to the rogue access point, all data transmitted over the Wi-Fi network passes through the attacker's device, enabling packet sniffing.

• **Traffic Monitoring**: Attackers use packet sniffing tools (like `Wireshark`, `tcpdump`) to monitor all data sent and received over the network, intercepting unencrypted traffic.

³³★★★³³

• **Sensitive Data Capture**: They can capture sensitive information transmitted in plaintext, such as login credentials, payment details, personal data, or session cookies if transmitted over unencrypted HTTP connections.

Goals of MITM Attacks

Stealing Sensitive Information: The primary goal is to intercept and steal sensitive information transmitted by users on the open Wi-Fi network. This includes
Login Credentials: Usernames and passwords for various online accounts if transmitted over unencrypted connections or intercepted through session hijacking.
Payment Details: Credit card information, bank account details, or payment processing data if transmitted over insecure connections.
Personal Data: Personal information, addresses, contact details, private messages, or other sensitive data transmitted over unencrypted channels.

Injecting Malicious Scripts (HTTP Traffic):
Attackers can also inject malicious JavaScript code into unencrypted HTTP traffic.
Malware Delivery: Injected scripts can redirect users to malware download sites, trigger drive-by downloads, or inject exploit code to infect devices with malware.
Session Hijacking: Malicious scripts can also be used for session hijacking, stealing session cookies and allowing attackers to impersonate users on websites or web applications.

Phishing and Credential Harvesting: Baiting Users for Credentials

Cyber-criminals can set up fake websites or pop-up pages within the open Wi-Fi environment to steal credentials directly from customers or employees.

Phishing Tactics on Restaurant Wi-Fi

Rogue Captive Portal (Fake Wi-Fi Login Page)
Attackers can create a fake captive portal page that users encounter when they try to connect to the restaurant's Wi-Fi.

Redirection to Fake Portal: When a customer or employee tries to access the internet through the open Wi-Fi, they can be redirected to a fake captive portal page hosted by the attacker (often through DNS spoofing).

Mimicking Restaurant Login: This page is designed to look like the restaurant's legitimate Wi-Fi login page, or a generic public Wi-Fi terms and conditions page.

Credential Request: The fake portal might ask users to enter credentials (e.g., email address, social media login, phone number, or even credit card information) in exchange for "accessing" the internet or using the Wi-Fi. This is a form of credential phishing.

Fake Login Pages (Pop-Ups or Redirects):
Attackers can inject malicious code (through MITM or compromised websites) to display fake login

³³★★★³³

pages as pop-up windows or redirects when users browse the internet on the open Wi-Fi.

Mimicking Legitimate Login Screens: These fake pages mimic login screens of popular online services (like Facebook, Google, Instagram, banking sites, email providers).

Credential Harvesting via Pop-Ups: Users are prompted to enter their login details in these fake pop-ups, believing they are logging into legitimate services. The entered credentials are then captured by the attacker.

Goals of Phishing Attacks:

Phish for Credentials: The primary goal is to phish for login credentials. Attackers aim to collect usernames and passwords for various online accounts.

Financial Exploitation: Credential phishing can lead to financial exploitation in several ways:

Restaurant Online Accounts: Credentials for the restaurant's online services (e.g., online ordering platforms, reservation systems, social media accounts, website admin panels) can be exploited to disrupt operations, deface websites, or steal business data.

Employee Business Tools: Credentials for employee accounts used for business tools (e.g., payment processing systems like Square, point-of-sale (POS) system access, accounting software) can be exploited to steal money, manipulate financial records, or gain access to sensitive business data.

Customer Account Credentials: In some cases, if customers use the open Wi-Fi to access their personal online accounts (banking, email, social media), attackers may attempt to phish for these credentials as well, although this is less direct to the restaurant business itself.

Malware Distribution (Drive-by-Downloads): Infecting Devices via Wi-Fi

Attackers on an open Wi-Fi network can take advantage of unpatched devices connected to the network to distribute malware. This can include ransomware, Trojans, spyware, or cryptojackers.

Malware Delivery Methods via Wi-Fi

Exploit Kits (via MITM or Malicious Websites):
Attackers can inject code into HTTP traffic (through MITM attacks on open Wi-Fi) to redirect users to websites hosting exploit kits. Alternatively, they can set up their own malicious websites and trick users into visiting them.
Exploiting Browser Vulnerabilities: Exploit kits scan users' browsers and devices for vulnerabilities (like outdated browsers, plugins, or operating systems).
Drive-by Downloads from Exploit Kits: If vulnerabilities are found, exploit kits can trigger drive-by downloads, automatically installing malware onto the user's device without their knowledge or explicit action.

³³★★★³³

Drive-by Downloads from Compromised Websites: If users on the open Wi-Fi network visit compromised websites (either intentionally or through redirects), they can be subjected to drive-by download attacks.

Infected Websites: Many websites are compromised and injected with malicious code that triggers drive-by downloads when visited.

Malvertising: Malicious advertisements (malvertising) on legitimate websites can also redirect users to sites hosting drive-by downloads or trigger downloads directly through malicious ads.

Social Engineering for Malware Installation: Attackers may use social engineering tactics to trick users on the open Wi-Fi into downloading and installing malware.

Fake Software Updates: Displaying fake pop-ups or notifications for software updates (e.g., for Flash, Java, browser updates) that look legitimate but are actually malware installers.

Enticing Downloads: Offering seemingly attractive downloads (like "free Wi-Fi speed boosters," "restaurant coupons," or "security tools") that are actually malware payloads.

Goals of Malware Distribution

Gain Access to Devices: Infecting devices with malware allows attackers to gain unauthorized access to customers' or employees' phones, tablets, or laptops connected to the open Wi-Fi.

Data Theft from Infected Devices: Malware can steal sensitive data stored on infected devices, including personal information, contacts, photos, documents, and financial data.

Install Remote Access Tools (RATs): Attackers may install Remote Access Trojans (RATs) to maintain long-term access to infected devices. RATs provide remote control, allowing attackers to monitor activity, steal data over time, or install further malware payloads.

Ransomware Deployment: In some cases, ransomware can be distributed via Wi-Fi attacks, encrypting files on infected devices and demanding ransom payments.

Session Hijacking: Impersonating Users Online

In a public Wi-Fi network, cyber-criminals can capture session cookies or tokens, potentially allowing them to hijack active user sessions on websites or web applications.

Session Hijacking Methods

Session Cookie Sniffing (Unencrypted HTTP): Attackers use
packet-sniffing tools (like `Wireshark`) to capture unencrypted HTTP traffic on the open Wi-Fi network.
Unencrypted Session Cookies: If users are accessing websites or web applications that use unencrypted HTTP connections (less common for

sensitive sites now, but still possible), session cookies transmitted in plaintext can be captured.
Impersonation with Stolen Cookies: Once session cookies are obtained, attackers can import these cookies into their own browsers and impersonate the user on the website, hijacking their active session.

Hijacking E-Commerce or Admin Sessions: If restaurant employees are logged into business-critical web applications or services (e.g., online ordering systems, payment gateways, restaurant admin panels) while using the open Wi-Fi, their sessions can be targeted.
Employee Login Sessions: Attackers aim to hijack sessions of employees logged into business accounts.
Access to Sensitive Systems: Hijacking employee sessions can grant attackers unauthorized access to sensitive business systems, potentially enabling financial theft, data breaches, or manipulation of business operations.

Goals of Session Hijacking

Access Business Accounts Without Passwords: Hijacking sessions of logged-in users allows attackers to access sensitive business accounts or services without needing to crack or phish for passwords. Session cookies serve as temporary authentication tokens.

Financial Theft or Data Breach: Gaining access to the restaurant's payment systems, databases, or customer data through hijacked sessions can lead

³³★★★³³

to financial theft (e.g., manipulating transactions, transferring funds) or data breaches (exfiltrating customer credit card information, order details, business records).

5. Rogue Access Point (Evil Twin) Attack: The Fake Wi-Fi Trap

As mentioned earlier, setting up a Rogue Access Point (Evil Twin) that mimics the restaurant's Wi-Fi network is a common tactic. This tricks customers into connecting to the attacker's malicious network instead of the legitimate one.

Evil Twin Setup

Network Name Spoofing (Same SSID): The attacker configures a fake Wi-Fi access point with the exact same SSID (network name) as the restaurant's Wi-Fi. For example, if the restaurant's Wi-Fi is named "RestaurantGuestWiFi," the attacker's rogue AP will also be named "RestaurantGuestWiFi."

No Encryption or Weak Encryption: Often, attackers set the fake Wi-Fi network to have no encryption (open network) or use weak encryption (like WEP, which is easily crackable). This makes it more attractive for users to connect to compared to a WPA2/WPA3 encrypted network, as it requires no password.

³³★★★³³

Stronger Signal (Potentially): The attacker's rogue AP might be configured to transmit at a higher power level, giving it a stronger Wi-Fi signal than the legitimate restaurant AP, making it appear as the more desirable option in Wi-Fi lists.

Goals of Evil Twin Attacks

Intercept All Traffic: All data transmitted by devices connected to the Evil Twin access point passes through the attacker's device. This gives the attacker visibility and control over all network traffic.

Data Interception and Theft: Attackers can intercept and steal sensitive data transmitted by users connected to the fake Wi-Fi network, including login credentials, personal information, payment details, and any other data sent over unencrypted connections.

Malicious Injection: Attackers can inject malicious payloads into the data stream, potentially infecting connected devices with malware, redirecting users to phishing sites, or manipulating web traffic.

6. Denial of Service (DoS) Attacks: Disrupting Restaurant Operations

A smaller restaurant heavily relies on internet services for various operations like online orders, payment processing, and customer communication.

33★★★33

Cyber-criminals can disrupt these operations by launching Denial of Service (DoS) attacks.

DoS Attack Methods

Targeting Wi-Fi Network (Wireless DoS):
Attackers can target the restaurant's Wi-Fi network directly, overloading it with traffic or disrupting its functionality.
Wi-Fi Flooding: Flooding the Wi-Fi network with excessive traffic using tools designed for wireless DoS attacks, like `MDK3` or `Aireplay-ng` (deauthentication attacks).
Wi-Fi Jamming: Using wireless jamming devices to interfere with the Wi-Fi signal, making it unusable.

Targeting Restaurant Internet Connection (Wired DoS): Attackers can target the restaurant's internet connection from external networks, overwhelming it with traffic.
Network Flooding (SYN Flood, UDP Flood):
Launching network flooding attacks (like SYN flood, UDP flood) against the restaurant's public IP address or internet gateway, consuming bandwidth and resources, making the internet connection unusable.
Application-Layer DoS (HTTP Flood): Targeting web servers or online services used by the restaurant with high volumes of HTTP requests, overloading the servers and making them unresponsive.

Goals of DoS Attacks

33★★★33

Disrupt Business Operations: DoS attacks aim to disrupt the restaurant's business operations by making their internet services unusable. This can have several negative impacts:

Online Order Disruption: Prevent customers from placing online orders, directly impacting revenue.

Payment Processing Issues: Disrupt online payment processing, making it difficult or impossible to accept card payments, affecting both online and in-person transactions if POS systems rely on internet connectivity.

Customer Service Impact: Disrupt online menus, websites, or communication channels, negatively impacting customer service and potentially damaging the restaurant's reputation.

Extortion (Potentially): In some cases, DoS attacks may be part of an extortion scheme. Attackers launch a DoS attack and then demand a ransom payment to stop the attack. This is more common with DDoS (Distributed Denial of Service) attacks, but even simpler DoS attacks can be used for extortion against small businesses.

Social Engineering Targeting Employees

Social engineering is a versatile and often effective tactic. Small restaurant employees, who may not have extensive cybersecurity training, can be particularly vulnerable to these types of attacks.

Social Engineering Attack Vectors

33★★★33

Phishing Emails (Targeting Employee Emails):
Cyber-criminals send deceptive emails to
restaurant employees, often targeting personal
email addresses if company emails are not easily
obtainable.

Impersonating Legitimate Entities: Emails might
impersonate legitimate vendors, customers,
suppliers, or even internal management.
Malicious Attachments or Links: Emails contain
malicious attachments (e.g., infected documents,
PDFs) or links leading to malware download sites
or phishing pages.
Trickery and Urgency: Social engineering emails
use trickery, urgency, or enticing offers to pressure
employees into clicking links or opening
attachments.

Pretexting (Impersonation Scams): Attackers use
pretexting, creating a fabricated scenario or
persona to gain trust and manipulate employees.
Posing as Service Technicians or Vendors:
Attackers might call or visit the restaurant
pretending to be IT support, maintenance
technicians, or vendors. They might ask employees
for information, access to systems, or to perform
actions that compromise security.
"Helpful" Assistance with Malice: They might
offer "helpful" assistance, like "fixing" a Wi-Fi issue
or "updating" software, but in reality, they are
installing malware or gaining unauthorized access.

Vishing (Voice Phishing - Phone Scams):
Attackers use phone calls (vishing) to deceive
employees.

³³★★★³³

Impersonating Trusted Authorities: They might call pretending to be from tech support, banking institutions, payment processors, or even government agencies (like tax authorities or health inspectors).

Requesting Sensitive Information: Attackers pressure employees to reveal sensitive information over the phone, such as login credentials, system passwords, payment processing details, or customer data.

Goals of Social Engineering Attacks

Credential Theft (Employee Accounts): Social engineering is often used to steal employee login credentials for various systems and services used by the restaurant.

Point-of-Sale (POS) System Access: Gaining access to POS system accounts is a high-value target, enabling financial manipulation and data theft.

Accounting Software Access: Access to accounting software (like QuickBooks, Xero) can allow attackers to manipulate financial records, steal financial data, or conduct fraudulent transactions.

Employee Databases: Access to employee databases can provide personal information for identity theft or further social engineering.

Internal Network Access

(Through Employee Devices): By compromising employee devices through malware installed via social engineering, attackers can gain a foothold in the restaurant's internal network.

Lateral Movement: Once inside the network, they can move laterally to other systems, targeting servers, POS systems, or back-office computers.

Malware Deployment Across Network: Employee access can be used to deploy malware, including ransomware, across the entire restaurant network, causing widespread disruption.

Physical Security Breaches: Direct Device Tampering

In addition to network-based attacks, cyber-criminals may attempt to physically gain access to the restaurant's devices, especially POS systems and back-office computers.

Physical Attack Methods

Device Tampering (POS Systems, Back Office): Attackers might physically access unattended or poorly secured devices within the restaurant.

POS System Tampering: POS systems are prime targets. Attackers might attempt to physically tamper with POS terminals during off-hours or when left unattended to install keyloggers, card skimmers (if applicable), or malware directly on the POS devices.

Back Office Computer Access: Back office computers, often located in less secure areas, can also be physically accessed to install malware, steal data, or plant backdoors.

USB Drops (Infected USB Drives): Attackers might strategically place infected USB drives in areas where restaurant employees are likely to find them and plug them into restaurant computers.
Infected USB Drives: USB drives are loaded with malware payloads, often disguised as legitimate files or documents.
Social Engineering via USB: Attackers rely on employees' curiosity or helpful nature to plug in the found USB drives into restaurant computers, leading to malware infection.

Goals of Physical Security Breaches

Direct Access to Systems: Physical access allows attackers to gain direct control over devices, bypassing network security measures.

Data Theft and Malware Installation: Physical access can be used to steal data directly from devices (e.g., copying files from POS systems or back office computers) or to install malware payloads, keyloggers, or backdoors.

Persistence and Long-Term Monitoring: Malware installed through physical access can provide persistence and long-term monitoring capabilities, allowing attackers to collect data or maintain access over time.

Prevention and Protection Measures: Strengthening Defenses

For a small restaurant, implementing robust security measures is crucial to mitigate the risks of these attacks. Here are key steps to take

1. **Secure Wi-Fi Network (Encryption)**: Avoid open Wi-Fi networks. Implement WPA3 or WPA2 encryption for the guest and business Wi-Fi networks. Require a strong password for Wi-Fi access. Consider separating guest Wi-Fi from the internal business network.
2. **Firewall Implementation**: Use a firewall to filter malicious traffic and control network access. Configure the firewall to block unnecessary ports and services.
3. **Endpoint Security Software**: Deploy endpoint security software (antivirus, anti-malware, EDR) on all devices, including POS systems, back office computers, and employee devices used for business purposes. Keep security software up to date.
4. **VPNs for Remote Access**: Use Virtual Private Networks (VPNs) for employees accessing business data remotely, especially when using public Wi-Fi or untrusted networks. VPNs encrypt communication, protecting data in transit.
5. **Regular Software and System Updates**: Regularly update all devices and software (operating systems, applications, POS system software, firmware) to patch known

vulnerabilities. Enable automatic updates whenever possible.

6. **Employee Security Education**: Educate employees about phishing attacks, social engineering tactics, Wi-Fi security risks, and physical security best practices. Conduct regular security awareness training.

7. **Disable Unused Ports and Services**: Disable open or unused ports and services on the restaurant's network and systems. Reduce the attack surface by minimizing unnecessary services.

8. **Physical Security Measures**: Implement physical security measures to protect devices and prevent unauthorized access. Secure POS systems, back office computers, and server rooms. Limit physical access to sensitive areas.

9. **Payment Card Industry (PCI) Compliance**: If the restaurant processes credit card payments, ensure PCI DSS (Payment Card Industry Data Security Standard) compliance. PCI DSS outlines security requirements for organizations handling credit card information.

10. **Regular Security Audits and Assessments**: Conduct regular security audits and vulnerability assessments to identify weaknesses in the restaurant's security posture and address them proactively.

By understanding these common tactics and implementing appropriate security measures, small restaurants can significantly improve their defenses

33★★★33

against cyber-criminals targeting their open Wi-Fi
networks and digital infrastructure.

Chapter 8 Beginner Cyber-Criminal Operations

For individuals starting out in cybercrime, operations tend to be relatively straightforward and low-risk. Beginners typically focus on methods that don't require advanced technical skills or extensive resources. These operations are often opportunistic, exploiting easily accessible tools, common vulnerabilities, and human error. They are designed to be quick, with minimal expertise required, and to avoid attracting excessive attention from law enforcement or cybersecurity professionals.

Phishing Campaigns

Phishing, even at a beginner level, is one of the most accessible and effective methods for cyber-criminals to exploit. It's a social engineering attack that relies on deception to trick victims into revealing sensitive information. While advanced phishing can be highly sophisticated, beginner phishing campaigns are often simpler but still effective.

Beginner Phishing Tactics

33★★★33

Email Spoofing (Basic): Beginner attackers use basic email spoofing techniques to make emails appear to come from trusted sources.

Simple Spoofing Tools: They might use online email spoofing websites or basic scripting tools to change the "From" address in emails, making them appear to originate from a legitimate organization (bank, online service) or a known contact. However, these basic spoofing methods are often easily detectable by email security filters.

Generic Phishing Emails: Beginner phishing emails tend to be more generic and less personalized compared to spear-phishing. They often use broad language and target a large volume of recipients rather than specific individuals.

Fake Websites (Simple Clones): Beginner attackers can create fake login pages or websites that mimic legitimate services, but often with less sophistication than advanced phishing sites.

Basic HTML Clones: They might use basic HTML copying and pasting techniques or simple website cloning tools to create replicas of login pages or website interfaces. These clones might be less polished and contain visual inconsistencies compared to advanced phishing sites.

Generic Phishing Pages: Beginner phishing pages often target widely used services like PayPal, Gmail, generic banking logins, or popular social media platforms.

Tools Used by Beginners

Social-Engineering Toolkit (SET - Basic Features): Beginners might use the Social-Engineer Toolkit (SET) to automate basic phishing tasks. SET offers features for crafting simple phishing emails and cloning websites. While SET has advanced capabilities, beginners often use its more straightforward phishing modules.

MailSpoof and Basic Email Spoofing Tools: Simple online email spoofing websites or basic scripting tools can be used to spoof email sender addresses.

Evilginx2 (Simplified Use): While `Evilginx2` is an advanced tool for bypassing 2FA, beginners might attempt to use simplified tutorials or pre-built configurations to launch basic `Evilginx2` phishing attacks, although effectively using its advanced features requires more skill.

Goals of Beginner Phishing

Steal Sensitive Information: The primary goal remains stealing sensitive information from victims.

Login Credentials: Harvesting usernames and passwords for email accounts, social media accounts, banking websites, or online services.

33★★★33

Banking Details: Stealing bank account numbers, credit card details, or PayPal login information for financial fraud.

Personal Data: Collecting personal information like names, addresses, phone numbers, or Social Security numbers for identity theft or further scams.

Gain Access for Further Exploitation: Phishing can be a stepping stone to gain initial access to victim accounts or systems for further exploitation.
Email Account Access: Gaining access to email accounts can be used for further spamming, contact harvesting, or accessing sensitive information within the email inbox.
Social Media Account Takeover: Taking over social media accounts can be used for spreading scams, malware, or phishing links to the victim's contacts.

Malware Distribution: Basic Payloads

Beginner cyber-criminals might venture into creating or deploying simple malware to infect machines. The malware used by beginners tends to be less sophisticated and often relies on readily available malware builder tools or basic trojan creation techniques.

Beginner Malware Tactics

Trojan Horses (Basic Creation): Beginners might attempt to create simple Trojan horse viruses disguised as legitimate files or software.

Virus Builder Tools (GUI-Based): They might use GUI-based virus builder tools or readily available online services that simplify the process of creating basic Trojans or malware. These tools often require minimal coding knowledge.

Disguising Malicious Files: They attempt to disguise malware as legitimate software, games, utilities, or email attachments to trick victims into downloading and executing them.

Ransomware
(Using Basic Ransomware Builders): Some beginners might experiment with ransomware, using basic ransomware builder tools or open-source ransomware code (like `Hidden Tear`) as a starting point.

Simple Ransomware Builders: Online ransomware builder services or basic ransomware creation tools make it easier for beginners to create rudimentary ransomware, although these often lack advanced features and might be easily detectable or decryptable.

Limited Customization and Features: Beginner-created ransomware often lacks sophisticated features like robust encryption, advanced evasion techniques, or professional ransom payment interfaces.

33★★★33

Tools Used by Beginners

Virus Builder Tools (Infostealer, njRAT - Basic Usage): Simple GUI-based virus builder tools, or basic Remote Access Trojans (RATs) like `njRAT` **(Using basic functionalities)**, can be used by beginners to create and deploy basic malware payloads.

Metasploit Framework (Basic Payload Generation): Beginners might use `Metasploit Framework` to generate basic payloads (like simple reverse shells or Meterpreter payloads) and deploy them, but often without deeply understanding exploit development or advanced evasion techniques.

Hidden Tear (Open-Source Ransomware): As mentioned, `Hidden Tear` and similar open-source ransomware projects might be misused by beginners as a base to create their own ransomware variants, although these are often not very effective in real-world attacks.

Goals of Beginner Malware Deployment

Gain Unauthorized Access to Victim Systems: Basic Trojans or RATs can provide beginners with unauthorized remote access to victim systems.

Remote Control (Limited): Beginner RATs often offer basic remote control functionalities, like file browsing, process management, or basic remote desktop access.

Data Theft (Basic): They can be used to steal basic data from infected systems, like files, documents, or browser history.

Ransomware (Limited Financial Gain): Beginner-level ransomware might be used for extortion, but its effectiveness is often limited due to simpler encryption methods and potential decryption vulnerabilities.

Credential Stuffing and Account Takeovers: Leaked Credentials

Credential stuffing is a relatively low-skill but potentially high-reward operation for beginners. It leverages publicly available leaked credentials to attempt automated account takeovers.

Beginner Credential Stuffing Tactics

Automated Attacks (Using Basic Tools): Beginners use automated bots and tools to attempt logging into multiple websites using leaked username-password combinations.

Password Lists from Data Breaches: They obtain password lists from publicly available data breaches, often found on dark web forums or paste sites. These lists contain millions of leaked usernames and passwords from previous data breaches.

Targeting Popular Websites: They target popular websites and online services, especially those known to have weaker security measures or a large user base where password reuse is likely.

Account Takeover (Limited Scope): If successful in gaining access to an account, beginner attackers might perform basic account takeovers.

Limited Exploitation: Beginner account takeovers are often less sophisticated, focusing on basic financial fraud or selling access to the stolen accounts.

Targeting Easily Monetizable Accounts: They might target accounts that are easily monetizable or can be used for quick financial gain, like e-commerce accounts, social media accounts with followers, or low-value financial accounts.

Tools Used by Beginners

Sentry MBA (Basic Configuration): `Sentry MBA` is a popular credential stuffing tool, and beginners might use its basic configurations to perform automated login attempts. However, effectively using `Sentry MBA`'s advanced features and bypassing sophisticated anti-bot measures requires more expertise.

Snipr or Proxy Networks (Basic Usage): Beginners might use basic proxy networks or free proxy lists to attempt to disguise their location and

33★★★33

evade simple detection measures on target websites, but often without understanding advanced proxy techniques or anti-detection methods.

Goals of Beginner Credential Stuffing

Access Accounts for Financial Fraud (Low-Value): Beginner credential stuffing attacks often aim for low-value financial fraud or quick gains.

Small-Scale Fraud: They might attempt to conduct small-scale fraudulent purchases using stolen e-commerce accounts or siphon small amounts of money from low-balance financial accounts.

Selling Stolen Accounts (Low Value): They might sell access to stolen accounts on dark web forums or to other cyber-criminals, but often at lower prices due to the lower quality or value of the accounts targeted.

Identity Theft (Limited): In some cases, account takeovers can be used to gather personal information for identity theft, but beginner operations are often less focused on sophisticated identity theft schemes.

Social Engineering: Exploiting Human Trust

Social engineering and scamming are beginner-friendly tactics as they primarily rely on manipulating human psychology rather than complex technical exploits. Basic scams, including simple phone scams (vishing), online scams, and lottery scams, are frequent activities for novice cyber-criminals.

Beginner Social Engineering Tactics

Vishing (Voice Phishing - Simple Scams):
Beginner vishing scams are often less sophisticated and rely on basic scripts or templates.

Generic Scam Scripts: They might use generic scam scripts or pre-written templates to make phone calls impersonating banks, tech support, or government agencies. These scripts often lack personalization and can be easily detected by wary individuals.

Requesting Basic Information: Beginner vishing scams often request basic sensitive information like credit card numbers, login credentials, or personal data over the phone, but may lack the convincing details and urgency of more advanced vishing attacks.

Lottery/Prize Scams (Basic): Beginner lottery or prize scams are often simple and easily recognizable as scams.

³³★★★³³

Generic Email or Message Blasts: They send out generic spam emails or messages claiming that the recipient has won a lottery or prize, requiring them to send money or personal information to claim their winnings.

Obvious Scam Elements: These scams often contain obvious red flags, like poor grammar, unprofessional formatting, and unrealistic promises of large prizes or winnings.

Romance Scams (Basic Online Dating Scams):
Beginner romance scams, often conducted on online dating platforms or social media, are usually less elaborate.

Basic Fake Profiles: They create simple fake profiles on dating sites or social media using stock photos or stolen images. These profiles might lack detailed personal information or consistent online presence.

Quick Relationship Building: They attempt to build relationships quickly online, often rushing into professions of love or emotional attachment to gain trust rapidly and start asking for money.

Goals of Beginner Social Engineering

Steal Money (Small Amounts): Beginner scams often aim to steal smaller amounts of money from victims.
Quick Cash Grabs: Lottery scams and vishing scams might aim for quick cash grabs, asking

victims to send smaller amounts of money for "fees" or "processing costs."
Lower Value Scams: Romance scams at a beginner level might target smaller amounts of money, seeking "loans" or "financial help" from victims rather than large sums.

Personal Information Theft (Basic Data):
Beginner social engineering can be used to steal basic personal information.
Data for Future Scams: Collected personal information might be used for future, more sophisticated scams or sold in bulk to other cyber-criminals.
Identity Theft (Basic): Stolen personal information can be used for basic identity theft activities, like opening fraudulent accounts or making small fraudulent purchases, but often lacking the sophistication of advanced identity theft schemes.

DDoS Attacks: Disruption for Chaos

Beginner cyber-criminals might engage in DDoS attacks to disrupt the services of small businesses or websites. DDoS attacks at a beginner level are often simpler and less sophisticated, relying on readily available booter services or basic DDoS tools.

Beginner DDoS Tactics

Botnets (Rental Botnets or Small-Scale):
Beginner attackers often use rented botnets or
small-scale botnets for DDoS attacks.

Booter Services (DDoS-for-Hire): They use paid
"booter" or "stresser" services, which are readily
available online. These services rent out DDoS
attack capacity for a fee, allowing beginners to
launch attacks without needing technical
infrastructure.

Small-Scale Botnets (Basic): In some cases,
beginners might attempt to create or acquire
small-scale botnets by infecting a limited number of
devices with basic botnet malware. However,
building and managing effective botnets requires
more technical expertise.

Basic DDoS Tools (LOIC): Beginner attackers
might use basic DDoS tools like LOIC (Low Orbit
Ion Cannon). LOIC is a simple tool that can
generate HTTP floods or other basic DoS attack
traffic. However, LOIC is often easily mitigated by
modern DDoS protection systems.

Targeting Small Businesses or Websites:
Beginner DDoS attacks often target small
businesses, individual websites, or less protected
online services that are easier to disrupt. They
might target:
Small Business Websites: Websites of local
businesses, restaurants, or small online stores that
may lack robust DDoS protection.

33★★★33

Gaming Servers: Targeting gaming servers to disrupt online games or for petty reasons.
Individual Websites or Blogs: Targeting personal websites, blogs, or forums for ideological reasons (hacktivism) or personal disputes.

Tools Used by Beginners

LOIC (Low Orbit Ion Cannon): A simple, open-source tool for launching basic DDoS attacks. Beginners might use LOIC due to its ease of use and availability, although its effectiveness against well-protected targets is limited.

Booter Services (Web-Based DDoS Tools): Web-based booter or stresser services are commonly used by beginners as they provide a user-friendly interface to launch DDoS attacks without requiring technical expertise.

Mirai Botnet (Variants or Public Code): While the original Mirai botnet was sophisticated, variants or public code snippets inspired by Mirai might be misused by beginners to attempt to launch botnet-based DDoS attacks, but often with limited success due to lack of expertise in botnet management.

Goals of Beginner DDoS Attacks

Disrupt Targeted Business or Service: The primary goal of beginner DDoS attacks is often simply to disrupt the targeted business or service.

³³★★★³³

Website Downtime: Causing website downtime for small businesses or online services, leading to loss of revenue or inconvenience to users.

Service Disruption: Disrupting online gaming servers or other online services, causing frustration to users.

Extortion (Limited Scope): In some cases, beginner DDoS attacks might be used for basic extortion, demanding small ransom payments to stop the attack. However, this is less common at a beginner level, and extortion attempts are often unsophisticated.

Hacktivism or Malicious Intent (Chaos): DDoS attacks might be motivated by hacktivism (disrupting services for ideological reasons) or simply for malicious intent, causing chaos and disruption for personal gratification or petty reasons.

Identity Theft and Fake Identities: Information Gathering and Simple Fraud

Beginner cyber-criminals might engage in identity theft by gathering personal information and using it to create fake identities for basic financial gain. Beginner identity theft operations are often less sophisticated and focus on simpler forms of fraud.

33★★★33

Beginner Identity Theft Tactics

Social Media Scraping (Basic Data): Beginners might scrape basic personal information from social media profiles or publicly accessible online databases.

Manual Data Collection: They manually collect publicly available information from social media platforms like Facebook, LinkedIn, Instagram, or Twitter, gathering data like names, dates of birth, addresses, and basic contact information.

Limited Automation: They might use basic web scraping tools or browser extensions to automate data collection from public profiles, but often without advanced scraping techniques or sophisticated data aggregation methods.

Fake Documents (Basic Creation): Beginner attackers create fake identities or documents, but often with less sophistication and easily detectable forgeries.

Simple Document Templates: They might use basic document templates or online tools to create fake IDs, driver's licenses, or utility bills. These documents often lack the security features and detail of professional forgeries.

Limited Forgery Skills: Beginner document forgeries are often visually less convincing and might be easily detectable by trained personnel or automated verification systems.

³³★★★³³

Phishing or Dumpster Diving (Opportunistic)
They might opportunistically collect additional personal information through basic phishing attempts or even physical dumpster diving, but these methods are often less organized and less effective than advanced information gathering techniques.

Goals of Beginner Identity Theft

Commit Fraud
(Simple Fraudulent Transactions): Beginner identity theft efforts often aim for simple fraudulent transactions.

Credit Card Applications (Basic): They might use stolen or fabricated identities to apply for basic credit cards or store credit accounts with lower credit limits.

Loans (Small Loans): They might attempt to take out small personal loans or payday loans using stolen or fake identities, but often targeting smaller loan amounts that are easier to obtain with less scrutiny.

Fraudulent Purchases (Low Value): They might make fraudulent purchases using stolen identities, but often targeting lower-value goods or services that are less likely to trigger fraud alerts.

³³★★★³³

Simple Website Defacement or Hacking (Basic Techniques): Ego and Reputation

Beginner cyber-criminals might hack into websites, often for simple website defacement, to showcase their "skills" or for ego-driven reputation within online hacking communities. Website hacking at a beginner level is often opportunistic and relies on easily exploitable vulnerabilities or misconfigurations.

Beginner Website Hacking Tactics

Exploiting CMS Vulnerabilities (Known Exploits): Beginners might target websites running common content management systems (CMS) like WordPress or Joomla and exploit known vulnerabilities in outdated versions or plugins.

Publicly Disclosed Vulnerabilities: They search for publicly disclosed vulnerabilities in CMS platforms or popular plugins and use readily available exploit code to target vulnerable websites.

Limited Exploit Development: Beginner attackers typically rely on pre-existing exploits and lack the skills to develop their own exploits for zero-day vulnerabilities.

Brute Force Attacks (Basic Tools): They might use simple brute-force tools to attempt to guess admin credentials of websites, often targeting default login pages or common usernames and passwords.

**Basic Brute-Force Tools
(Hydra - Simple Usage):** They might use basic password-cracking tools like `Hydra` with default configurations or simple dictionary lists to attempt brute-force attacks against website login forms or SSH services.

Limited Evasion of Security Measures: Beginner brute-force attacks often lack sophisticated techniques to evade account lockout mechanisms, CAPTCHA systems, or IP blocking implemented by websites to prevent brute-force attempts.

SQL Injection (Basic Exploitation): Beginners might attempt basic SQL injection attacks, often using automated tools or simple SQL injection payloads, but without deep understanding of SQL injection vulnerabilities or advanced bypass techniques.

Automated SQL Injection Tools: They might use automated SQL injection scanning tools or basic SQL injection payloads to test for vulnerabilities in website input fields.

Limited Payload Complexity: Beginner SQL injection attempts often involve simple payloads and might not be effective against well-secured websites or web applications with robust input validation.

Goals of Beginner Website Hacking

Website Defacement
(Ego and Reputation): The primary goal is often to deface websites.

Simple Defacement Messages: They might deface website homepages by replacing content with simple messages, hacker tags, or symbols to showcase their "achievement."

Hacker Reputation (Online Communities): Website defacement can be motivated by ego and the desire to gain reputation within online hacking communities or among peers.

Steal Sensitive Data (Limited Scope): In some cases, beginner website hacking might aim to steal sensitive data.

User Login Details (Basic Databases): They might attempt to steal user login details from website databases if they can gain access through vulnerabilities like SQL injection. However, data theft is often secondary to website defacement for beginners.

Credit Card Information (Less Common): Stealing credit card information from websites is less common at a beginner level and requires more advanced skills and access to vulnerable e-commerce platforms.

Crypto Mining: Resource Hijacking for Minor Gains

Beginner cyber-criminals might engage in basic cryptocurrency mining or cryptojacking, using other people's computers or networks to mine cryptocurrency without permission. Beginner cryptojacking operations are often simpler, less efficient, and might focus on less detectable browser-based methods.

Beginner Crypto Mining Tactics

Browser-Based Crypto Mining (JavaScript Injection): Beginners might inject malicious JavaScript into websites or distribute malware that secretly uses the victim's computer resources to mine cryptocurrencies through their web browsers.

JavaScript Code Injection: They might inject cryptojacking JavaScript code into compromised websites, forums, or online platforms. When users visit these infected websites, the JavaScript miner runs in their browsers, using their CPU power to mine cryptocurrency.

Simple Cryptojacking Scripts: Beginner cryptojacking scripts are often basic and might be easily detectable by browser security features or antivirus programs.

³³★★★³³

Malware Infections (Basic Miners): They might infect devices with basic crypto mining malware, often distributed through simple Trojans or drive-by downloads.

Simple Miner Malware: Beginner mining malware is often less sophisticated and might be easily detectable by antivirus software.

Limited Efficiency and Stealth: Beginner miners might be less efficient in terms of mining performance and might lack advanced stealth techniques to hide their presence or avoid detection by security monitoring tools.

Goals of Beginner Crypto Mining

Use Others' Computing Resources (Minor Cryptocurrency Gains): The primary goal is to use others' computing resources to mine cryptocurrencies.

Small-Scale Cryptocurrency Mining: Beginner crypto mining operations often yield only minor cryptocurrency gains due to limited resources, basic mining techniques, and potential detection and removal of miners.

Passive Revenue Generation (Low Effort): Crypto mining, even at a beginner level, can provide a form of passive revenue generation with relatively low effort, as the mining process can run automatically on infected systems. However, the profitability is often marginal compared to more sophisticated cybercrime operations.

³³★★★³³

Conclusion: Low-Skill Operations, Real-World Consequences

For beginner cyber-criminals, operations are often basic, relying on well-established methods, publicly available tools, and exploiting easily accessible vulnerabilities and human error. The motivations are often financial gain, ego, or causing chaos. While these crimes may be less sophisticated than advanced cyber-attacks, they can still have serious consequences for victims, ranging from financial loss and data breaches to service disruptions and identity theft. Even beginner cyber-criminals can cause significant damage, highlighting the importance of basic cybersecurity hygiene, awareness, and defense measures to mitigate these common threats.

Chapter 9 A Beginner Cyber-Criminal Operation:

Step-by-Step Breakdown

To illustrate how a typical cyber-criminal operation unfolds, especially one conducted by a beginner, this chapter provides a step-by-step breakdown of a simple attack targeting a small business or individual. This operation will outline the common stages, tools, and techniques used, from initial reconnaissance to the final monetization phase.

Step 1: Reconnaissance & Information Gathering - The First Look

Before launching an attack, even a beginner cyber-criminal understands the importance of reconnaissance. Gathering information about the target is crucial for planning and executing the attack effectively.

Actions in Reconnaissance Phase

1. **Social Media Scraping (Basic)**: The attacker starts by reviewing publicly available information on social media platforms like Facebook, LinkedIn, or Twitter.

³³★★★³³

2. **Manual Profile Review**: They manually review profiles of individuals or businesses, looking for easily accessible details like names, email addresses (often listed publicly), job roles (for targeting employees), or basic contact information.

3. **Limited OSINT Tools**: Beginners might experiment with basic OSINT tools like `theHarvester` to gather publicly available data from search engines and online sources, but often use these tools in a limited or unsophisticated manner.

Domain Information (Basic Lookup): The attacker might perform basic WHOIS lookups to gather information about a target company's domain, such as domain registration details, contact information associated with the domain, or publicly listed email addresses.
Online WHOIS Tools: They use online WHOIS lookup websites to query domain registration databases.

Network Scanning (Simple `Nmap` Scans): The attacker might run simple network scans on the target's IP address or domain using basic `Nmap` scans.
Basic Port Scans: They use `Nmap` to perform basic port scans, checking for common open ports like 80 (HTTP), 443 (HTTPS), 22 (SSH), or 3389 (RDP) on the target system or network.
Limited Scan Options: Beginner scans often use default `Nmap` scan types and lack advanced scan techniques or in-depth vulnerability analysis.

33★★★33

OSINT
(Open Source Intelligence - Basic Search): The attacker will also perform basic searches for any publicly leaked data related to the target, using search engines or simple breach data search sites.

Generic Web Searches: They use search engines like Google to search for publicly leaked data, credentials, or mentions of vulnerabilities related to the target business or individual.

Have I Been Pwned? (Basic Check): Beginners might use `Have I Been Pwned?` to check if any email addresses or domains associated with the target have been involved in known data breaches.

Goal of Reconnaissance

Gather Basic Information: The goal is to gather enough basic information to design a targeted attack, identify a potential entry point, or find an easily exploitable vulnerability. The information collected is often limited and readily available publicly.

Step 2: Initial Contact: Phishing or Social Engineering - The Hook.

Once basic reconnaissance is complete, the beginner attacker initiates initial contact, often using phishing or simple social engineering tactics to trick the target into taking an action that compromises security.

³³★★★³³

Actions in Initial Contact Phase

Phishing Email (Generic or Slightly Targeted):
The attacker creates a phishing email, often generic or only slightly targeted.

Basic Phishing Templates: They use basic phishing email templates, often readily available online or in tools like SET, with generic language and less personalization.

Spoofed Sender Address (Simple Spoofing):
They use simple email spoofing methods to make the email appear to come from a trusted entity (bank, online service, colleague), but often without sophisticated spoofing or email authentication bypass techniques.

Malicious Link or Attachment (Generic): The email contains a malicious link leading to a fake login page or a malicious attachment (infected document, executable). These malicious elements are often generic and might be easily flagged by security filters.

SMS Phishing (Smishing - Basic): If the attacker has obtained a phone number (e.g., from social media or public listings), they may use SMS phishing (smishing) tactics, sending a malicious link via text message.

Generic SMS Templates: They use generic SMS templates with basic phishing messages, often impersonating delivery services, banks, or online platforms.

Malicious Link in SMS: The SMS message contains a malicious link to a phishing website or a malware download site.

Phone Phishing (Vishing - Basic Script): In some cases, a beginner cyber-criminal might attempt phone phishing (vishing), using a basic script or template.

Pre-written Scam Script: They use a pre-written scam script or template to guide their phone conversation, impersonating tech support, bank representatives, or government agencies.

Requesting Simple Information: They ask victims to reveal sensitive information over the phone (credit card numbers, login credentials, personal data) or to perform actions that compromise security (downloading remote access software).

Goal of Initial Contact

- **Trick the Victim into Action**: The primary goal is to trick the victim into taking some action, like clicking on a malicious link, opening an infected attachment, or revealing sensitive data over the phone or through a fake web form.

³³★★★³³

Step 3 The Breached: Gaining Access - Basic Exploits or Malware.

Once the victim has been tricked into taking the desired action, the attacker attempts to exploit the situation to gain access to the victim's system or accounts. This often involves deploying basic malware or exploiting simple vulnerabilities.

Actions in Exploitation Phase

**Malware Installation
(Simple Trojan or Keylogger)**: If the phishing attempt leads to malware installation, the attacker deploys a basic Trojan or keylogger.
Basic Trojan Payloads: They deploy simple Trojan payloads, often created using virus builder tools, that provide basic remote access or data theft capabilities.
Keylogger Deployment: They might deploy simple keyloggers to capture keystrokes and steal login credentials, using readily available keylogger software or basic keylogging techniques.
RAT Deployment (Basic in some cases, beginners use basic Remote Access Trojans (RATs) like `njRAT` or `DarkComet` (using basic functionalities) to gain remote control over the victim's machine, although using RATs effectively requires some technical understanding.
Credential Harvesting (Fake Login Pages): If the phishing attempt successfully directs the victim to a fake login page, the attacker harvests the login credentials entered by the victim.

Credential Capture from Phishing Forms: They capture usernames and passwords entered into fake login forms on phishing websites and store these credentials for later use.

Exploiting Unpatched Vulnerabilities (Known Exploits - Basic Use): In limited cases, if the attacker identified easily exploitable vulnerabilities in the target system (e.g., through basic `Nmap` scans), they might attempt to use known exploits, often using `Metasploit` in a very basic manner.

Basic `Metasploit` Exploitation: Beginners might use `Metasploit Framework` to launch basic exploits against known vulnerabilities, but often without deeply understanding exploit mechanics or advanced post-exploitation techniques.

Goal of Exploitation

Gain Basic Access: The goal is to gain basic access to the victim's system, network, or online accounts. This access is often limited and might not provide full control or advanced capabilities.

Step 4 Escalating Privileges - Staying at User Level

Beginner cyber-criminals typically do not focus on privilege escalation techniques. Their operations often remain at the user level of access gained in the initial exploitation phase. Privilege escalation requires more advanced technical skills and exploit development knowledge, which are usually beyond the scope of beginner operations.

33★★★33

Actions in Privilege Escalation Phase (Typically Skipped or Limited)

Limited Privilege Escalation Attempts: Beginner attackers may make limited attempts at privilege escalation, often relying on basic misconfigurations or easily exploitable vulnerabilities, but without sophisticated techniques.

User-Level Access Maintained: In most beginner operations, the attacker remains at the user level of access initially gained. They operate with the privileges of the compromised user account and do not actively pursue administrative or root-level access.

Goal of Privilege Escalation (Limited)

Limited or No Privilege Escalation: The goal of privilege escalation is often not actively pursued by beginners. They typically operate within the constraints of user-level access.

Step 5 Data Collection or Exfiltration - Gathering the Prize

Once inside the victim's system, the beginner attacker starts collecting data, but often using basic and less sophisticated methods.

³³★★★³³

Actions in Data Collection/Exfiltration Phase

Stealing Basic Files (Manual File Browsing):
The attacker might manually browse through the compromised system's file system, searching for easily identifiable sensitive files.
Manual File Search: They manually search for files in common user directories (Documents, Desktop, Downloads) looking for files with names suggesting sensitive content (e.g., "passwords.txt," "bank statements," "financial records").
Limited Data Search Scope: Beginner data collection is often limited to easily accessible and readily identifiable files, without advanced data mining or search techniques.

Exfiltrating Data (Basic Transfer Methods): If they find data to exfiltrate, beginners use basic and often insecure methods to transfer the data to their own systems.
Email Exfiltration: They might email stolen files to their own email addresses, often using unencrypted email protocols.
Cloud Storage (Basic Uploads): They might upload stolen data to free cloud storage services like Google Drive or Dropbox, but often using unencrypted uploads or without advanced anonymization techniques.
Unencrypted FTP or HTTP: In some cases, they might use unencrypted FTP or HTTP to transfer data to their own servers, exposing the data in transit.

³³★★★³³

Goal of Data Collection/Exfiltration

Steal Basic Data for Monetization: The goal is to steal basic data that can be quickly monetized or used for simple fraudulent activities. The data collected is often less sensitive or of lower value compared to advanced data breaches.

Step 6 Persistence Short- Term Access

Beginner cyber-criminals typically do not focus on establishing sophisticated persistence mechanisms. Their operations are often short-term, opportunistic, and do not prioritize maintaining long-term access to compromised systems. Persistence techniques require more technical expertise and knowledge of system administration, which are often lacking in beginner operations.

Actions in Persistence Phase (Typically Skipped or Limited):

Limited Persistence Attempts: Beginner attackers might make minimal attempts at persistence, often relying on simple backdoors or basic autorun mechanisms, but without robust or stealthy persistence techniques.
Short-Term Access Sufficient: In most beginner operations, short-term access is sufficient to achieve their immediate goals (data theft, basic fraud), and they do not prioritize maintaining long-term persistent access.

³³★★★³³

Goal of Persistence (Limited)

Limited or No Persistence: The goal of persistent access is often not actively pursued by beginners. Their operations are typically short-lived and opportunistic.

Step 7 Covering Tracks and Evading Detection - Minimal Stealth

Beginner cyber-criminals make minimal efforts to cover their tracks or evade detection. Their focus is often on quickly executing the attack and monetizing the results, with less concern for long-term stealth or advanced anti-forensics.

Actions in Covering Tracks / Evading Detection Phase (Basic)

Basic Log Deletion (Limited Scope): The attacker might attempt basic log deletion, but often in a limited and unsophisticated manner, only deleting obvious logs or browser history, without understanding comprehensive log management or forensic analysis.

Limited Anonymization (Basic VPNs): They might use basic VPN services or free proxy lists to attempt to anonymize their IP addresses and hide their location, but often without understanding advanced anonymization techniques or using Tor or more robust VPN solutions.

Goal of Covering Tracks/Evading Detection

Basic Evasion Efforts: The goal of covering tracks is often limited to basic evasion efforts, primarily aimed at avoiding immediate detection or simple tracebacks, but without sophisticated anti-forensics or stealth techniques.

Step 8 Monetizing the Attack - Simple Methods, Low Revenue Payoff

Finally, the beginner attacker monetizes their attack using simple and often less lucrative methods.

Actions in Monetization Phase

Ransomware Deployment (Basic Ransom Demands): If they have deployed ransomware, they demand a ransom payment for decryption, but often with basic ransom notes and less professional payment processes.
Selling Stolen Data (Low-Value Data Sales): Stolen data is often sold on dark web forums or to other cyber-criminals, but at lower prices due to the

lower value or quality of the data and limited sales channels.

Fraudulent Transactions (Small-Scale Fraud): If banking information or credentials have been obtained, the beginner attacker might attempt to conduct small-scale fraudulent transactions, make unauthorized purchases, or transfer small amounts of money from compromised accounts.

Account Sales (Low-Value Accounts): Stolen accounts (social media, e-commerce) might be sold on underground forums or account marketplaces, but often at lower prices due to the lower value or limited usefulness of these accounts.

Goal of Monetization

Low Revenue, Quick Gains: The goal is often to achieve low revenue and quick gains with minimal effort and risk. Beginner cyber-criminal operations are often not designed for large-scale financial profit or long-term sustainability.

Simple Operations, Real-World Impact

This step-by-step breakdown illustrates how even a beginner cyber-criminal can execute a basic operation, utilizing readily available tools and techniques. While their methods are often unsophisticated and their operations less complex than advanced cyber-attacks, they can still cause real-world harm to individuals and small businesses. Understanding these basic attack patterns is crucial for implementing foundational cybersecurity defenses, educating users, and mitigating the risks posed by even low-skill cyber-criminals.

33★★★33

Cyber-Security

This "Hackers Hand Book" has aimed to demystify the world of cybercrime, unveiling the tactics, tools, and strategies employed by cyber-criminals, from beginners to sophisticated groups. We've explored the multi-phase nature of financial data theft, the cybercrime arsenal, the threats to mobile devices, the dual-use nature of publicly available security tools, the creation of malicious websites, and the vulnerabilities of small businesses. We've also examined the operations of beginner cyber-criminals, highlighting their methods and limitations.

www.ez-web.ca

33★★★33

Key Takeaways

Cybercrime is a Structured Operation: Financial data theft is not random; it's a structured, multi-phase operation involving reconnaissance, exploitation, data exfiltration, and monetization.
Diverse Cybercrime Arsenal: Cyber-criminals have access to a diverse array of tools and resources, ranging from dark web marketplaces to open-source hacking tools and ransomware-as-a-service.
Phishing and Social Engineering Remain Key: Despite technical advancements, phishing and social engineering attacks remain highly effective, exploiting human vulnerabilities to bypass security controls.
Publicly Available Tools Misused: Many publicly available security tools designed for ethical hacking are repurposed for malicious purposes by cyber-criminals.
Phones are Vulnerable Targets: Smartphones are increasingly targeted by cyber-criminals, and understanding mobile security threats and defenses is crucial.
Small Businesses are High-Risk: Small businesses, especially those with open Wi-Fi and limited security resources, are particularly vulnerable to cyber-attacks.
Beginner Cybercrime is Accessible: Even individuals with limited technical skills can engage in basic cybercrime operations using readily available tools and techniques.

Moving Forward: Building a Stronger Defense

Understanding the cyber-criminal mindset and their methods is the first step in building a stronger defense. To stay ahead in the cyber security game, both individuals and organizations must:

Prioritize Security Awareness: Continuous security awareness training and education are essential for users at all levels. Emphasize the importance of recognizing phishing attacks, practicing safe online behavior, and understanding social engineering tactics.

Implement Layered Security: Adopt a layered security approach that combines technology, processes, and people. Implement robust security controls at all levels, including firewalls, intrusion detection systems, endpoint security, multi-factor authentication, and data encryption.

Keep Software Updated: Maintain up-to-date software and systems. Regularly apply security patches for operating systems, applications, and firmware to mitigate known vulnerabilities.

Embrace Proactive Threat Intelligence: Leverage threat intelligence feeds to stay informed about emerging threats, attacker tactics, and indicators of compromise. Proactive threat intelligence helps in anticipating and mitigating potential attacks.

Strengthen Wi-Fi Security: Secure Wi-Fi networks with strong encryption (WPA3 or WPA2) and avoid open Wi-Fi networks, especially for business operations. Segment guest Wi-Fi networks from internal business networks.

Focus on Incident Response and Recovery: Develop robust incident response plans and data backup and recovery strategies. Effective incident response and recovery capabilities are crucial for

minimizing the impact of cyber-attacks and
ensuring business continuity.
Continuous Learning and Adaptation: The cyber
threat landscape is constantly evolving. Continuous
learning, adaptation, and proactive security
measures are essential to stay ahead of
cyber-criminals and maintain a strong security
posture.

A Final Word of Caution

The information provided in this book is for educational and defensive purposes only.

Engaging in any form of hacking or cybercrime is illegal and unethical.

This book is intended to empower you with knowledge to protect yourself and your organization, not to facilitate or encourage illegal activities.

Always use this information responsibly and ethically, within the bounds of the law and with respect for the security and privacy of others.

By understanding the tactics of cyber-criminals, implementing robust security measures, and fostering a culture of security awareness, we can collectively build a more secure digital world and protect ourselves and our organizations from the ever-evolving threat of cybercrime.

33★★★33

About the Author

An aspiring tech innovator, I'm deeply engaged with the fields of AI, coding, web development, and cybersecurity. I'm captivated by the potential of these technologies to solve complex challenges and transform our world. My ambition is to leverage my skills to design and build impactful solutions that contribute meaningfully to people's daily lives and a better future.

This book leverages the capabilities of AI to compile and structure information on cybercrime. While AI assisted in the drafting process, the content has been meticulously fact-checked and validated by human experts in the field. Our focus is on providing you with a reliable and informative guide. The true value of this book comes from the verified content and its potential to educate and protect readers against cyber threats.

Mathæs Danıɛl

33★★★33

```
01010101  01101110  01101100  01101111
          01100011  01101011
00100000  01110100  01101000  01100101
          00100000  01010011
01100101  01100011  01110010  01100101
          01110100  01110011
```

33★★★33

The Hackers Hand Book

www.ingramcontent.com/pod-product-compliance
Lightning Source LLC
LaVergne TN
LVHW062317060326
832902LV00013B/2265